Warren Burton

Helps to Education in the Homes of our Country

Warren Burton

Helps to Education in the Homes of our Country

ISBN/EAN: 9783337228149

Printed in Europe, USA, Canada, Australia, Japan

Cover: Foto ©Paul-Georg Meister /pixelio.de

More available books at **www.hansebooks.com**

HELPS TO EDUCATION

IN THE

HOMES OF OUR COUNTRY.

BY

WARREN BURTON,

AUTHOR OF "THE DISTRICT SCHOOL AS IT WAS."

BOSTON:
CROSBY AND NICHOLS,
117, WASHINGTON STREET.
1863.

The most difficult as well as the most important work on earth is the wise education of children. Parents, will you kindly accept the following counsels from a sincere and earnestly devoted friend? May they make good, in some appreciable degree, the homely Saxon word placed first on the titlepage!

Opportunity is now taken to explain to friends, that, during the last two years, infirm health has kept me from the educational field in which I had been exclusively working for ten years before; or rather it has prevented me, to my keen regret, from the more urgent duty of devoting myself, in some active way, to our present momentous cause. In the mean time, as strength would allow, and with many intermissions, this volume has been under preparation. It is, I trust, a worthy service of the Christian patriot to provide, even in a small measure, against future adversities, public and private, in our beloved country, by laboring at those more hidden sources of good and evil which lie in the shadow of its homes.

W. B.

CONTENTS.

	Page.
LECTURE ON PARENTAL RESPONSIBILITY	3
LECTURE ON GOVERNMENT, MISGOVERNMENT, AND NO GOVERNMENT IN THE FAMILY	27
LECTURE ON THE MANAGEMENT OF THE SELFHOOD	65
PASSAGES FROM A LECTURE	115
I. Gifts	117
II. Bad Companionship	120
III. Irritability of Temper	123
IV. Children at Table	127
SUGGESTIONS ON THE DISCIPLINE OF THE OBSERVING FACULTIES	135
A LETTER FROM THE AGENT OF THE MASSACHUSETTS BOARD OF EDUCATION	274
TOPICS OF RELIGIOUS EDUCATION	277
THE FIRST KNOWLEDGE OF THE CREATOR	279
THE FIRST AND GREAT COMMANDMENT	293

	Page.
The Child's First Ideas of Jesus	335
The Bible	344
Notes	357
Index	359

NOTE. — The general heads of this volume hardly give a fair view of its contents. The Index, at the close, shows the items of interest to be exceedingly numerous, and of great variety.

LECTURE

ON

PARENTAL RESPONSIBILITY.

NOTE.

THE statements and considerations in the following Lecture are of the most serious moment : indeed, their importance can hardly be overrated. Yet the hackneyed title and topic, it is feared, will at once affect many with a sense of dulness and discouragement, and cause them to hasten beyond to what may seem more inviting. In anticipation of this, a special and earnest request is ventured, that such persons would at least make an attempt at reading. The old subject is here presented in a manner somewhat new ; and it is humbly hoped that the reader will be interested and impressed beyond what might be expected from so trite a theme. If the perusal could be made without haste, so as to permit to words their fullest force, the little longer time taken would hardly be regretted. This preliminary discourse, so read, would almost necessarily better prepare the mind for the practical instructions which follow.

LECTURE

ON

PARENTAL RESPONSIBILITY.

THE chief purpose of this world is the formation and development of man. Here he not only commences existence, but prepares for another world. In the present condition of things, this preparation is difficult: many think it to be doubtful. The human being, as now constituted, is, indeed, fearfully as well as wonderfully made. He is a mysterious system of capabilities and possibilities. He is capable of good, and capable of evil. He may be happy, or he may be unhappy; indeed, exceedingly joyous in felicity, or at the utmost extremity of wretchedness. He can answer to the various epithets of virtue and piety given in the Sacred Word; or he may make applicable to himself, in different degrees, one and another, and even many, if not all, of those terms by which sin against God, crime against man, and the depravity of the heart, are expressed. To particularize: First, as a little child, or the larger youth, in the family of his birth, he may be a precious delight by his dispositions, so affectionate and generous, and, by his manners, so gentle and winning. In school he may be studious and orderly; on the play-ground, ingenuous, sweet-tempered, and beloved. Next, as an apprentice or a clerk, he may be respectful, diligent, honest. Then, as a neighbor and a citizen, he may be upright, obliging, peaceable, public-spirited. As a husband and a father, he may make his home the best emblem and image of very heaven. Toward the Divine Being he may be reverent and loving, deeply but cheerfully pious. In short, he has within his capacities that by which, the Holy Spirit helping, he shall be able to love God with all his heart, and his neighbor as himself. This world may be better and happier for his single life in it, and heaven at length be more blessed for his single added presence there. Such is the human being capable of becoming, if he shall be properly cared for, wisely trained, adequately educated.

But now to particularize the opposite capabilities and possibilities: This same human infant has that within him, by which, in his parental abode, he may be ill-tempered and disobedient; a very furnace of selfish passions, consuming his own best good, and the peace of his nearest, truest friends. At school he may be idle, unruly, impudent, rebellious; on the play-ground, unfair, testy, rough, vulgar, profane. Let him become an apprentice at a trade, or a clerk in a store; and what then? — unfaithful, disobedient, disrespectful, truthless, rakish. He may purloin from his employer to pay for finery, dainties, and other extravagances. At length, he may sink into dissipation and various dissoluteness, and early die, — a human ruin. But suppose him apparently to recover from his sensual and spendthrift habits. He may now enter the field of business for himself, to do what? To cheat his customers, to live on others' losses. Again: as a neighbor, he may be rude, crabbed, disobliging, unfeeling. As a citizen, he may possess scarcely a single spark of public spirit. Self — hard, dark, unheavenly self — is the centre and the circumference of all the hopes, fears, aspirations, activities, and satisfactions of his life. But his home, — should he enter on married and parental life, — what the possibilities here? Ah! by sharp-spoken petulance, or lowering sullenness, or by fierce outbursts of anger, by niggardliness or tyranny, by intemperance and other depraved indulgences, this choicest, innermost spot may be made like unto that outer place of darkness, and weeping, and gnashing of teeth.

Furthermore : standing beside man's infancy, and contemplating the future, we may in all truth affirm, that possibly he shall plunge into direst crime, — shall steal, rob, murder. Yes, that little being, who has, as yet, not entertained a purpose, a feeling, or a thought of wrong; who seems, in his present weakness and innocence, utterly incapable of inflicting any sort of pain on others,— that now absolutely harmless creature may, at twenty or thirty years of age, enter your window in the darkness of midnight, and, during the helplessness of your sleep, grope his way to your goods or your money; and should you perchance be aroused, and attempt to defend your property, he may stab or shoot you dead on the spot; then murder your agonized, shrieking wife, to prevent her alarming the neighborhood at the instant, or identifying his person afterward as the perpetrator of the crime. Ah! language fails to depict the horrible atrocities which lie within the capabilities and possibilities of the man. This world may be much worse for his having lived in it; and the world to come,— the all-seeing Eye alone can trace his path, and discern his state, in its labyrinthine and endless depths. Along such a line of tendencies, along such a course of immorality, vice, crime, enormity, or, at least, through some one portion or another of it, this human infant is likely to run, should he be neglected, — should he not be properly trained, wisely, adequately educated. Is it not a momentous alternative? There is alarm, there is terror, in the very thought of the contingency.

But this is God's own child. Does he leave him unprovided for, and to his own poor, feeble self? Oh, no! his providence is most faithful. Out of all the rest of the world's inhabitants he provides one man and one woman, who are to be the very first, the long-continuing, and the most responsible guardians under himself. Of all finite beings, they are nearest in place, nearest in blood, and nearest in affection. In them, indeed, has been implanted an instinctive, peculiar love, not primarily as an especial gratification to them, but as insuring fidelity to the paternal Creator, and to this his offspring. Thus to the earthly father and mother is committed the most dependent and the most impressible of all animated things. They have in their hands the beginnings of a boundless destiny, folded up as in a bud. They have in charge the wondrous, the auspicious opening. The Lord God Almighty calls and sets apart these two to this duty, as much as if he pointed down to them with a visible finger, and spoke in articulate thunder in the presence of an assembled world. It is the highest, the most holy, calling of their lives. They are to be the surest of all protectors, the earliest and the most influential of all educators. They are to fit this being for noblest virtue and loving usefulness in the present life. They are to act sooner and to do more than all others to fit him for the life to come. They are not only to teach and train, but to rule as in a realm. God's vicegerents, they are seated on the strongest throne beneath all the skies: this throne is the earliest and tenderest heart, the first, sweet, enduring love, of a little child. If faithful to their gentle sceptre, all the armies of earth, all the hosts of hell, cannot move them therefrom: they are next in power to the Almighty. Thus, more than all others beneath the heavens, they are the arbiters of time and eternity to this immortal spirit. Such is the responsibility of parentage.

Now, can it be, that in this age of unparalleled mental light, and amid all its various Christian institutions, these God-commissioned guardians, guides, and rulers shall not understand their office, and feel their obligations? Can it be that *they* shall not be faithful?

Let us see. In human affairs, knowledge and skill are considered necessary to success. Preparation and qualification are requisites well appreciated all the world over. Who thinks of entering on the chosen avocation for a livelihood or for usefulness, without forethought and preparation? Let us glance at a few instances. Suppose one of the so-called learned professions: what years has the aspiring youth been qualifying himself for this! What book after book has he plodded through, what expense incurred, and possibly what severe privations endured, to place himself at the commencement of his favorite, life-long career! Another devotes himself to some department of the arts. Whatever his genius, he most patiently persists and works on long, before he reaches the lofty mark of his burning desire. Still another gives himself to some one of the material interests. He spends years upon the soil, learning how crops and cattle are matured, and turned to best account; or in a shop or manufactory, to obtain the craft of wielding tools or of tending machinery whereby inanimate matter is moulded into forms of use; or in some mercantile warehouse or common store, acquiring a knowledge of such productions, and a facility in selling them. Indeed, from the highest profession down to the lowest handicraft, there is preparation. Custom requires, necessity commands it. Without it, unless there be extraordinary talent, there must be failure of success. The very child understands this fact, and expects, as he grows up, to leave, it may be, the dear home of his birth, to learn the occupation of his life.

Again: consider a young woman. She is a distinct and providential part in the great order of things. She is to take a commanding position in the passing but momentous procession of human lives. She also has been spending years in preparation for the future. She has passed through the schools, studying at least the common branches, and perhaps the various higher matters in literature and science,—Latin, French, and the abstruser mathematics. She must be an adept at pencil-drawing, and also painting. Moreover, for months, it may be for years, she is a pupil at the piano, that she may touch the keys with even respectable skill. Perchance, she is versed in household affairs; at least, well understands general arrangements and the more delicate mysteries of the culinary art. With all these acquirements, if there be judicious regard to time, talent, taste, and life's important duties, no fault can be found.

At length, such a young man and such a young woman give themselves to each other in sacred marriage. Here is a new home. Home! it is earth's most precious place. It is that one spot which heaven most nearly touches, and which its messengers soonest and oftenest visit. The spirit of God broods over the home. The Creative Power descends, and there is a new human being; something utterly unknown to time, space, or finite intelligence, before; something distinct from all other existences that ever were, or will be; something the exact like of which is not, and never will be, in the whole universe of God. It is committed to the charge of this twain. From a thousand millions these two are separated by the Creating Hand, and ordained as primary and especial ministers, to keep, and to keep most safely; to educate, and to educate most wisely; to bless, and to bless more than all the rest of the world, particularly in the first years,— this creature of the Most High.

Well, those who have spent so long a period carefully fitting themselves for occupations which have to do with chance-coming strangers, and which operate simply on the more general needs of family and social life,— they, surely, cannot but have qualified themselves for this duty, one nearest to the hands, most solemn to the conscience, and closest, dearest to the heart. What books must they have read, what treatises studied! How have they consulted the experience of living persons around! How have they humbly sought wisdom from above! If they ever did pray, they must have earnestly supplicated now. *They* cannot but be ready to do time's noblest work on earth's loftiest, lordliest product. What! are they not Heaven's own angels embodied in the flesh? Alas, alas! that young father and that young mother have spent not a year, not a month, not a week, not a day, not an hour,— they have not read a book nor made an inquiry,— in preparation. Some foresight and provision for the merest physical necessities make the only exception. They take the central instrument of the grand orchestra of creation, framed and toned by the Infinite Artist into almost utterly unskilled hands. What can ensue but that it should be loosened or strained into discords, or even shattered to ruin, and scattered, as it were piecemeal, to the world's tempests?

This may be looked upon with some degree of indulgence, considering the thoughtlessness and rushing impulses of youth. But these parents go on to more mature and sober life, and child after child — it may be, numerously — is at length intrusted to their care, with immeasurable destinies rooted in the earliest and most impressible years; and yet nothing is intentionally and specifically done to repair that lack of fitness with which they assumed the parental office in the beginning. Is it any wonder that families are what we so often see, — misrule at the head, and misdeeds in the members? How can it be otherwise than that boyhood should be ill-tempered and disobedient at home; disorderly at school; contentious, unmannerly, vulgar, and profane in the street; and perhaps take early steps toward dissipation and ruin? What more likely than that sister girlhood should grow up self-willed, petulant, vain, frivolous, and self-idolizing? Is it any wonder that communities are shattered by petty self-interests, and imbittered by scandals; and that ordinary business, in which Christian justice and kindness should prevail, is one hot war of struggling, yea, crushing antagonisms?

There are supposed to be thirty thousand human beings, once innocent babes at the maternal bosom, now shut up within the granite walls and iron doors of the prisons of our country. Is this any wonder, when we take into view the homes from which they came, and the pupils of other homes among whom they fell? Is it any wonder that as many more, quite or almost as wicked, are yet abroad, desolating society? Is it any wonder that all around, and in every grade of life, there are low sensualities, fiery passions, destructive collisions, and all the multiform shapes and methods and innumerable complications of unheavenly selfishness? Yes, yes: why should not all these things be? for who puts the rush of causes back from their inevitable effects? Oh! when I perceive, in so many directions, intelligent, reasoning, interest-seeking men and women, inquiring into and clearly understanding and surely acting on the philosophy of cause and effect in all the concerns of life but that of the right care and culture of those nearest and dearest to them in their homes, it seems a strange, unaccountable fatuity, a stupendous insanity. Behold, notwithstanding countless instances in the past, and numerous cases in the present and all around, admonish, and that even terrific gulfs of ruin close by send up the wail of those perishing down in them; notwithstanding God's Holy Word majestically commands and tenderly pleads, and his retributive providences awfully warn,—how many, by their own direct example, incite their children, or at least, by their neglect, permit them, to approach, step by step, the brink of the deep, dark, fatal abysses; yea, and perhaps they stand by, apathetically, senselessly, and see them drop, one by one, in! Ye saints and angels, who gaze down in pity or amazement, is not this a madness?

Consider the other various interests of life: how numerous the appliances to promote their advancement! What institutions, books, periodicals, meetings, discussions! As for reading, the publications come, the whole year through, almost as thickly as do the flowers in the few vegetative months; and some of them rival, in richness and beauty, the very flowers. How bright the centre-table with its gilded volumes!

In the houses of the wealthy is the large and various library; and, in the hands of all, the multifarious newspaper. From the unwholesome places of teeming brains creeps that vermin, that reptile literature, which steals into the hands of brothers, thence into those of sisters, and into the hearts of both, leaving vileness — it may be, poison — there. But in how few of these houses, take the land through, from the lowest to the highest, do we find a single volume teaching the Heaven-commissioned heads of the household how to train up their children in the way they should go! There are such books, there are periodicals, for this purpose; but the booksellers affirm, that of all the works of common, practical value, they have the least call for treatises on family discipline.

What gatherings all over the land, for discussion, knowledge, and impulse in respect to the increase and management of property, and the multiplying of facilities for business! What exhibitions, emulations, successes, and applauses! There are agricultural fairs and cattle-shows: and the land glows with culture, and gladdens in the beauty of flowers and the ripeness of fruits, and proudly swells with the largeness and fatness of kine.

Of conventions, there are other than those of patriotism and partisanship: there are horse conventions, and even poultry conventions; and men and women, and beauty and fashion, collect around in multitudes to behold and admire. Our most gifted orators are invited on such occasions, and they sound their most silvery eloquence in the cause of brutes and vegetables. But who ever heard of a similar gathering of fathers and mothers, in loving ardor and conscientious anxiety, to learn from each other, by interchange of ideas, by the discussion of questions, and by the hearing of committee-reports, how to rear and educate noble sons and daughters; how to prevent sons from descending, as so many have done, beneath the brute; how to prevent daughters from coming to be not much better than inactive vegetables,—yea, than very weeds; how to make the infant a fully developed man, worthy to be earth's powerful lord, and heaven's blessed heir?*

---

* The maternal associations which have been instituted in many churches are no exceptions to what is intimated above. These are confined to one sex, are of limited numbers generally, and of vacillating and feeble operation. So I have been informed by many pastors. The meetings for educational discussion, mentioned toward the close of this volume, had not been started when this lecture was first written; and they are now but an experiment and a beginning.

In case of physical defect, how anxious are parents for a remedy! Let there be only a stain marring personal beauty, and they would apply steel or fire, with all the pain, if thus the blemish could be taken out, and no scar left. How little is thought of the stain made by bad companionship and example on the soul! I knew a mother who travelled a hundred and fifty miles in the cold, cheerless winter, carrying her infant for a distinguished surgeon to set aright its distorted foot; and who then journeyed back again, all unaccompanied, except by strangers, to an impoverished home. Is there any mother who would not do the same, or a father who would not give his last dollar, to save a child from life-long lameness? But with what moral distortions do children come into the world, and these inherited from parents themselves, or more remote progenitors! yet how few parents are anxious about, or even at all notice, such obliquities! Take these obliquities in the beginning, how soft and pliable to heaven-directed management! Let them alone, they become crookednesses, gnarled, knotted, enduring, perhaps hideous to the sight, and an anguish to the bosom, of that community which is obliged to hold them in its midst.

But some reply, "We have been faithful to *our* children: *we* have diligently sought and practised the best methods of culture." But have you done all your duty? Your children are still insecure, unless your neighbors are as faithful as yourselves. You must not rest till all around partake of your spirit, and co-operate in your action. Society is like one great jellied mass: touch but a single spot, and it trembles throughout. Is your son a pupil at the public school? Is he a member of the street-community of boys? If so, he is every day exposed to the contagion of vice. Unless his ears shall be stopped like the deaf, he cannot but hear vulgarity and profanity; catch words and ideas, too, which shall sink into his memory, and infuse a stain into his soul, which perhaps, through the eternal ages, may not be cleansed out. Your daughter may be as pure as a snow-flake just from the airy cloud, or as the sweetest blossom of the spring; yet she is surrounded and endangered by influences that may defile and deform the crystalline threads, and the fresh, delicate bloom, of her soul. There are those in polished society, and perhaps altogether unsuspected, whose very presence is almost a poison. Ah! whose son or daughter is safe with the present morals of cities, towns, and villages? Yet who is alarmed at this condition of things, or seeks to alarm others? Let a pestilence, let the cholera, sweep along the land, and approach, day by day, nearer and nearer, and what consternation! How the authorities bestir themselves! How cellars and drains are looked into, searched closely, and cleansed! Not the speck of a decaying vegetable must remain. Indeed, were some offensive matter unexpectedly discovered in a neighbor's yard or in the contiguous street, sending its effluvia into the premises of the most aristocratic gentleman, and, if the laborer could not be hurried to its removal, he would himself seize the spade with his own soft, white hands, — yes, so would the mother of his children, however delicate and high-bred, — and dig a pit, and thrust the nuisance in, and bury it up, to save the dear ones from the pest-inviting atmosphere. But the elements of a moral cholera are as thick in the great cities as the smoke and soot that lower over their roofs: indeed, they pervade every town and village of our land. But who stirs a limb or utters a word toward an active and determined purification?

The angel of death often snatches little children away to the care and training of heavenly teachers; while infatuated parents put forth all their puny strength, and shriek out supplications, to prevent this most blessed rescue from their own destroying hands: but let the demons from the bottomless pit come stealing up, come rushing up, and there is no alarm, and they seduce and destroy at their pleasure.

How long shall the proper care of infancy, the nurture of childhood, and the guidance of youth, be deemed a small, petty business, and utterly unworthy special consideration, amid what are called, or what are fancied to be, the great affairs of life, — money-making, dress, dress-displaying, and pleasure-seeking? A small matter, a petty matter, is it, — the early dispositions, tendencies, and habits of the human being, which unfold into angelic beauty, or burst out into horrible deformity! Yet the parents who thus feel and believe, or at any rate who neglect the higher nature, call in, when a child is seized with sickness, the most reliable physician within their means; and, learned and eminent as he may be, he stoops to the small business of feeling the infantile pulse, of counting throb by throb, and of keenly inspecting the color of the tongue. An unusual tinge upon the skin is then of consequence: it is a symptom. But be assured, that there are little things, yea, least things, in the earliest character, too generally unheeded, which are also symptoms,— spiritual symptoms; and, to the wise and watchful educator, they are most fearfully premonitory. Little and belittling is it,— the charge of the chief and central organism of this lower creation, around and for which the wheels of nature turn and its springs play in all their mightiness and minuteness, and for which wondrous providences have been displayed, and even nature-rending miracles wrought! — the charge of it, that it may be unfolded into beautiful order, and grand and joyous activities, and be made to sing for ever in unison with heavenly spheres!

For this immortal one, the spiritual mansions were builded, glorious, boundless, eternal; yea, for him the third heavens may have been lifted up, nearest to the light inaccessible. But, alas! through causes, commencing with the earliest life; yea, by the sharp-cutting consequence of undirected thought, ungoverned appetites, burning passions, and motives yet closer within the will and the self-hood, and still more intensely ungodly,— he may prepare, year by year, in his own mysterious, unfathomable nature, an ever-deepening, terrific hell; and none but the Omniscient can know when or whether such awful industry shall ever stop or pause. To save such a being from himself, the Ancient of days, the "I am that I am," descended into Immanuel,— Jehovah into Jesus. Yea, the most merciful Father continues long-suffering and ever-providing. Nevertheless, how utterly without avail may it be, unless those who receive body and soul from his immediate hand and spirit, and are left in living freedom, shall fulfil their initiatory, far-reaching, superlative part!

LECTURE

ON

GOVERNMENT, MISGOVERNMENT, AND NO-GOVERNMENT IN THE FAMILY.

NOTE.

This and the following Lecture were given at first extemporaneously. It was of great importance to make the subject interesting; for, of all topics presented to the public ear, that of family education seemed to be the most dull and uninviting. It was desirable to show that there was no lack of life and spirit in it; that, while it was of the first moment, it could also be made somewhat attractive. Illustrative incidents were, therefore, quite numerously introduced. It was found that those which had been witnessed by the lecturer, and especially those in which he himself had borne a part, were the most effective on the audience. These Lectures, when put on paper for delivery, retained the same characteristics. They are now presented in print, much in the same style. The first personal pronoun continues to be used where the incidents were really of a personal character. This circumstance, it is believed, cannot but impart to them a reality and an impressiveness which a more abstract, and apparently more modest, method would not have afforded. It is therefore hoped that this individual prominence of the writer will not be set down to the account of any thing like egotism; for nothing could be further from the truth. The object has simply been to come as close to minds and hearts as possible, for the sake of doing them good. It may be said here, moreover, once for all, that if, anywhere in these productions, the author makes himself personally conspicuous, this is done for the sake of greater use or convenience, and not at all for self-exhibition.

LECTURE

ON

GOVERNMENT, MISGOVERNMENT, AND NO-GOVERNMENT IN THE FAMILY.

IN the first place, let us understand the grounds of parental power and filial submission. It is only according to certain laws, certain fixed methods of matter and spirit, that the plans of the Divine Father can be fulfilled. The human being comes into the world in utter ignorance of these conditions of welfare. Hence, from very birth, he is liable to infringe them and to suffer. First, he knows not what will do him bodily injury; so he must be forcibly restrained. In this simple circumstance of safety begins the trial of what is called "government." A child's hand is withheld from a sharp knife, or burning lamp, or some other destructive agent; and he is thus initiated into submission to a power above himself. No one, having the care, would fail to exercise the due control, in case of positive and immediate danger. At this point, however, determined, inevitable government often ceases. From this point there may be continued a course of obedience, order, quietness, comfort, peace, in the parental and filial relations; or, on the other hand, there may commence long-protracted disobedience, disorder, distraction, and any thing but peace. The child was made for activity: it is absolutely necessary for his growth and health; also for his mental as well as his physical development. So, in his instinctive impulses, he betakes himself this way or that, and gets hold of one thing or another. He knows not the tendencies of his conduct in respect to a hundred things and movements. The work-basket which he might pull from the stand, or the plate he might draw from the table, are not valuables to him. He knows not why he may not touch them, as well as try his strength or perceptions on any thing else. He has no idea, moreover, of property as belonging to others. Why should not he appropriate scissors or muslin just as others do who have eyes and hands? He is a little, crawling, creeping, picking, pulling, pushing, climbing, tottling, and tumbling-down piece of activity.

What is denominated "mischief" in the household vocabulary is his work; and this sort of industry is really of incalculable profit in his education. Nevertheless, he must be permitted to go exactly so far, and no farther; to do exactly so much, and no more. He must be governed. Authority must be made absolute. It must exercise compulsion in all these instances, just as much as in the case of closely threatening physical danger. Then there was no hesitation, whatever might be the resistance, the angry wilfulness, and even spasmodic contortions, of the little operator. Begin at the earliest, and keep straight on, and it will not be difficult, generally, to establish certain rules of action with a child, and to make him understand that these rules must be obeyed the same as he obeys the necessity of not touching fire. It simply requires watchfulness and firmness. Here is a practical illustration which fell under my own eye many years ago. A little boy of nine months old is making the tour of the room on all fours; stopping at this thing, then at that; tugging at a chair, pushing a cricket, and poking along something else; but, coming within reach of the bright-headed but black-footed implements of the fireplace, he stops, and turning his little face over his left shoulder, and his bright eye up to his mother, who happens to be behind at the opposite side of the room, he gives her a significant look, as much as to say, "I should like to know how those things feel, and to use them as you do, mother. But you needn't worry: I shall mind you, and not touch them." Then, turning back, he pushes his travels among unforbidden curiosities. There was the same habit of contented obedience to other necessary restrictions. Yet this was an uncommonly sickly and nervous child by constitution; one who, by indulgence, would have been a screeching, scratching little rebel, driving at every thing that was accessible, like thousands of others, in spite of anybody or any thing but irresistible strength or impenetrable matter.

In many families, however, rules are made only to be overruled or to be unmade. In fact, the household sovereign, who does not insist on immediate submission to separate and incidental commands, is likely at length to fall into a weakness of character, which will not insist on a uniform compliance with what are intended to be the fixed statutes of the domestic realm. Places for certain things, and times for certain doings, which should be regular, — the proper where and when,— get all askew, and are sometimes lost beyond recovery. Yes, laws, which are important to the safety and the life of the heedless little ones, will be broken over and broken over, until, in consequence, some terrible calamity shall smite that home with sadness, or even with agonizing bereavement. Such has been the occasion of many a fall, breaking the limbs; and many a drowning in the forbidden water.

Sometimes such parents are conscious of their error, and, indeed, are even intending reform; but they get no farther toward it than intention. Said a mother of this character to her pert little boy, "George, I tell you what it is: I'm going to turn over a new leaf with you."—"Mother," was the reply, "I tell *you* what it is: you have been a great while turning over that new leaf, but haven't got it over yet." Alas! how many there are, who, like this impotent one, are always intending to turn over the new leaf, but never get it over; or, if they do, the leaf will not stay *put*, but flits back, and exhibits the same continually repeated tale of weakness, misrule, and discomfort!

Here the remark is well in place, that it is those children who are ever breaking the laws of home, or in whose homes there are no laws to be broken, who come to be the offensively vicious and the destructively criminal. Such, of a certain class, are often sent on long voyages, under strict sea-captainship, to Calcutta or Canton; or on a three-years' cruise to look on and see how monstrous whales are taken in the South seas or on the North-west coast. But, if the unmanageable fellows belong to a certain other class, their voyage is a short one, and hard enough to bear: it is from the court-room to the House of Correction or the State Prison.

If the child shall be trained to conform to established rules, then he will be much more ready to obey those commands and injunctions arising from exigencies which are ever new. In the first place, in a little child's impulses and activities, he is liable to take directions in which no established rule of prohibition will come in his way. Household affairs are various and changing; and the child must be in the midst, with his little eyes to look, his little hands to take hold of, and his curiosity to be gratified. Well, the prohibition to be given is the first one of the kind, and may never occur again. But if it is not made, if his hands are not held back, he does harm to himself or to something else. If he is not restrained in this particular instance, much less can he be restrained in the next necessity of the sort: so there will be incalculable disorder. Indeed, where a child shall not be made implicitly to obey particular commands, it will be hard to make him conform to general rules. It will be difficult to establish any general law for him. He has his own will in these individual instances, in spite of the authoritative injunction: what will he care, then, for the wish, the word, the command, that he shall not go anywhere and do any thing that he chooses? Let it be understood, then, that general rules of government begin in special directions which are continually made necessary in family life. These are as rivets, ever thickening, which keep up the bars and barricades of physical and moral safety about the home.

A most successful parental educator, whose large family of children did him distinguished honor, was once asked the secret of his success. The patriarch replied, that he had no great wisdom to boast of, but that he would simply state one circumstance which might have had an important bearing on the matter. His children could never remember the time when they did not obey their father and mother. The principle thus illustrated has been intimated before, and is of infinite importance: it is to begin to establish authority over the child as soon as any restraint is needed, and to keep this authority unbroken. Of course, the occasions must occur so early, that no human remembrance could go so far back as to reach them. Recollection, as it runs along back to the earliest, to the faintest thought, finds a father and a mother who were never disobeyed. With such training, and such habits thus early formed, there cannot ordinarily come the struggle of the great will with the little will, and — what we sometimes hear about — the absolute necessity of breaking the will. For the will has always been submissive and pliant. It has been thoroughly habituated to yield to the strong, the knowing, the careful, the tender, yet the firm and majestic authority which has, from the first, bent above it. How, with such wise management, would the child be saved from disagreeable memories of the uprisings of its own will, and the down-pressings, yet unsteady pressures, of the superior will! If the parent only knew it, it is absolute cruelty to a child to bring on such conflicts by the let-alone policy, and thence to fill the mind with ever-living prickles from the keenly vivid remembrance of such passages in child-life.

What folly, then, is there in the notion, often expressed, that children should never be made to obey until they understand the reason why! When, according to this theory, they are old enough to obey, they are, for the most part, quite too old to do it according to their own ideas. Children draw inferences much earlier than is commonly supposed. Appertaining to this very point, here is an illustration which I myself received from a father's own lips. A lady, conversing on the methods of education and the proper time of beginning discipline, pointed to his own little boy, with the remark, "Such children are not old enough to mind." After she had gone, the father gave the child some trivial direction; and he straightened up his bit of a body, and turned up his tiny face, with a sort of newly-felt consequence, and exclaimed, "Father, I'm not old enough to mind!"

By a glance at the methods of God in introducing his children into the world; at his wise and beautiful laws appertaining to the commencement and the progress of the human faculties, — the weakest reason, one might think, would perceive the course of duty. See how things have been pre-arranged! A child is put into the hands of the parent in baby and total weakness both of body and mind; and this, that authority may *not* be deferred, but, on the contrary, be most firmly established, at the earliest activities of life. How beautifully adapted is one thing to the other! An infantile lack of animal strength is set over against an infantile ignorance of mind and a blind impulsiveness of will. The feeble creature is not only entirely in the keeping, but under the absolute control, of his authoritative friends. At first, they can hold him as with the strength of a single nerve. Being present and observing, they can restrain him from any ordinary danger. But they acquire a power over him beyond that of muscular strength: deeper and more subtle causes affect his will, and lead him to submit. There is a reverence, a commingling of fear and love. Besides this, there is a sort of sentiment of duty. He soon begins to feel that he *should*, as well as that he must, yield obedience. Here, indeed, is the first dawning of conscience. Then comes in habit. From his earliest recollection, he has been accustomed to yield to this authority; and, if his governors and guardians have been faithful, it is, at length, with him as it is with most good citizens in regard to the laws of the State: there is no thought or wish to violate them.

Let the habit of obedience be thoroughly confirmed, and the child, who at first needed painful compulsion, will afterwards want only rational, tender, but unwavering guidance. The power of parents, and of their coadjutors around, together with reverence and an unfolding conscience within his soul, all conspire to make him a peaceful subject of the first and most sacred empire on earth, — that of the home. Now, could such a state of things be brought about there, how obedient, respectful, and orderly would grow up the communities of youth in the school, of manhood in the neighborhood, and of citizenship in the town and the state! But it is not always so; and why? Because these first rulers, these most responsible of all monarchs, do not faithfully perform their duty. They do not designedly neglect; but they are inadvertently delinquent. Indeed, many, who well understand the nature of their responsibilities, are ignorant of the true methods of meeting them. Instinct may impel, tender parental affection may prompt, them to be faithful; but, after all, family government is a science and an art, and they have not the endowment. There are natural gifts about it, as there are in the government of a school or of a country. Some have them, and they can hardly help governing. Others (and they seem to be a numerous class) are not so favored: they need instruction and a sort of training for their office. Indeed, those who in their very nature can govern, as it is called, may be much assisted by hints drawn from the experience and observation of others.

It must be confessed, that an irreverent, unruly spirit has come to be a prevalent, an outrageous evil among the young people of our land. Foreigners observe the fact, and are very much struck — are indeed shocked — by it. An elderly clergyman related to me this incident: "The Persian bishop, who visited this country several years ago, called on me; and I introduced my daughter. His very first words, accompanied by a kindly look, were these: 'Do you obey your parents?'— as much as to say, 'Can it be, that a young lady, so intelligent and well-mannered as you appear to be, is, like American children and youth in general, disobedient and disrespectful to parents?'" The clergyman asked the bishop if he intended to visit England on his return home. He replied, that he could not then tell: he must, in the first place, write home, and obtain his father's consent. The bishop's father was an ecclesiastic of an inferior grade, and actually subordinate to the son. But, as a *parent*, he was considered far superior in position and office. Thus he must send across two oceans to obtain that parent's consent before he could make a passing call on gloriously renowned England. The incident shows a world-wide distance between the East and the West in other things than longitude.

Some of the good old people make facetious complaint on this deterioration of youthful character and manners. "There is as much government now as there used to be in our young days," say they; "only it has changed hands." There are certain professional men, who have occasion to know, above most others, into whose hands it has been transferred: for instance, physicians, ministers, and school-teachers.

Many other people, of less extensive acquaintance, have been convinced of the fact.

"This is a democratic country, there is not the least doubt," remarked a jocose friend; "for the *majority* — that is, the children — do govern." Surely they have it mostly all their own way. Yes, the democratic spirit has crept into the home, where it was never intended to be. Father and mother — those sovereigns by divine right — have been deposed. Alas for morals and order until there shall be a restoration! It should be laid down and inculcated through the nation as a great maxim of civil and political wisdom, that sound family monarchies are the surest foundation of a steadfast and a happy republic.

Instinctive parental love — that special endowment from the Divine Parent — is the first preparatory qualification for the holy office; but it is quite often perverted into a disqualification. This was intended to insure fidelity to the child's best good; but how frequently does it lead to blind, destructive indulgence! The loving instinct of the brute makes it faithful, but never spoils the offspring. Would that the same could be said of the human sovereign of the brute!

This abuse of instinctive tenderness is particularly shown in a lack of firmness to resist a child's importunities. The darling craves some improper gratification. His parent, true for the moment to conscience, says, "No;" but the child's experience is, that *no* is turned to *yes* by half an hour's teasing. So he takes to this peculiarly melodious sort of eloquence: "Now, do, mamma: I say, won't you? Do let me have it!" till the conscientious, the womanly, yea, the faithful motherly "No" is whined clear out of his way; and the mamma often comes very near to something much like whining too: "Yes, you may have it: but, my child, how you *do* trouble me! it seems as if you would wear my very life away." But, from a different disposition, the reply is, perhaps, "Yes: take it, and be off!" If such a mother desires her child's love, let her understand that he is certainly not growing in affection during this uncomfortable space between refusal and compliance. He is irritated by the delay. His thought and feeling are, "Why do you keep me waiting? Let me have it now. You know you'll let me have it by and by, after I have teased long enough; as you always do. I don't like you, mother; I don't like you, old mother! Let me have it now." Such is the secret language of his soul. Well, does he like her any better after she has come round, or rather down, to his little mightiness? Not at all. He thinks of her, cares for her, no more, till he comes back for some new indulgence; sure, moreover, that he shall get it. The child, whose appetites and passions are thus developed, really loves less than any other one. His lower nature is made to overgrow and cover up and crush down his higher; until, at length, it takes a good deal of perforation and probing about to get at what little heart he has left.

Again: the parent wishes her child to enjoy life; to be a happy child. How often she bends her back, hardens her hands, and scorches and withers her face, to furnish luxuries for his pleasure! Yet she is taking the most direct and certain means to counteract her heart's earnest desire; namely, that he should enjoy life. He is a spoiled child; and the spoiled child is one of the most wretched beings that ever disappointed the purpose of creation. The least opposition stirs up his irascible temper; and is such a disposition a blessing? Brothers and sisters and men-servants and maid-servants, if there be such unfortunates about him, must go quick at his bidding, or spring and get something at his yell. How he will hop and stamp and flutter, and shake himself about, if he cries "Go!" or "Come!" and nobody starts! He gets provoked at things inanimate just because they retain their natural qualities: the nail his cap clings to, or the door which sticks a little in the opening, have to take instant punishment; or, rather, the little fist that hits them a blow has to take it. But alas for those that are not inanimate, and who can feel!

The school-mate who will not turn down the way that suits him, or rather, perhaps, who will not stop by the way, or not do something else, just as he demands, becomes a momentary victim, and has to take a push, pinch, or kick. And what is he at school? — a self-willed, insolent nuisance to the teacher; selfish and petulant with the pupils; by turns, an offence to everybody. It is he who comes home knitting his brows, grating his teeth, and muttering his wrath, perhaps his hate, against some one. It is most likely to be the teacher. It is he who makes the teacher's good appear nothing but evil before the parent; and, alas! that parent, spoiled also, has not the justice and the good sense, not the common sense, to go to the teacher, and hear his account of the matter: no; but rather repeats and propagates the child's misstatements. At length arise gross calumnies and intense bitterness; and sometimes, especially in country towns, comes the breaking-up of the school itself, sometimes of neighborly peace besides. These spoiled children are absolute robbers. Do they not compel the teacher to leave his duty to others to take care of them? Do they not wrest time and teaching from the whole school? And why not? Look into that family den whence these depredators have issued forth, and their felonious characters are at once accounted for.

Let us now just glance at a contrast. Here is a child to whom "No" has always been *no*. The negative, once put down, stays, unless there shall be some peculiar change of circumstances. He has been trained never to be impatient. He has learned to confide in the love and the wisdom which cross his inclinations. Well, his request is refused; what then? He drops not a tear, says not a word, but away he trips to something else, — to his work, his books, or his play. He skips like a lamb, he capers in the breeze, he carols like a bird, — a happy boy still, the well-governed and trustingly obedient son of a wise parent, — God's best angel in the flesh.

Verily, these weak parents spend absolutely more time in running after and coaxing, and *trying* to govern, their children, ten times over, forty times over, than the judicious disciplinarian. Said an excellent lady, whose grandchildren were of the sort described, "Oh! if my daughter had not so much to do, she would have time to train her children." I could have told her, that the very reason why her daughter did not have time to train her children was because she had not, in good season, taken time to train them. Her neglect led to misrule; and this misrule compelled her, at length, to attempt to rule at a great expense of time, strength, and patience, and, after all, with but little success. To what wretched shifts are such imbeciles sometimes driven! How often are methods adopted which the plainest common sense might perceive to be the immediate antecedents of evils worse than those which are sought to be prevented!

Not a few resort to stratagem, to downright deception. The consequence is, the quick-eyed child soon sees through the trick. He reads the natural, unbidden language of the tone and the countenance, contradicting the words; and he receives a lesson in deception, — indeed, in falsehood, — which he will practise back again: yea, he will pay off his parent for such profitable instruction by lying, and with compound interest.

Others — God's vicegerents though they are, with absolute authority, and sufficient strength to enforce it — humbly pay for permission to exercise a rightful control. They hire their liege subjects to obey. Ah! what promises of rides, sights, plays, playthings; or, what is worse, of pie, cake, candy, — any thing that shall pervert still more an already perverted palate, and weaken even further an already weak sense of duty! — for this is the consequence. These domestic rulers flatter themselves, that by these means they have exercised due authority, — have secured obedience. But this is not authority or obedience: it is a bargain, the benefit of which is mostly on one side. The child thus trafficked with and tempted will practise his first Yankee shrewdness on his own parent. He will wait and wait, and wind up the purchaser to the point at which the pay suits him, before he will close in. Thus he exchanges obedience for what, in business, is called a "valuable consideration;" or, to use another mercantile phrase, he performs a "pretty little operation"— on his own father or mother. What an absurdity! The Almighty God's own nearest agent, possessing an adult body, equipped with two strong arms and two capable hands, and having this very God and his Holy Word, and also conscience and common sense, in support, — what an absurdity, what a sin, to stoop down, *down*, to buy up, not obedience, but tardy compliance, of tiny weakness! Alas! how will even wisdom sometimes change suddenly to folly, and substance and strength fall into very nothingness, in this matter of government! While delivering lectures on domestic education, I was once the guest of an excellent lady. She was a very mother in her own little Israel, and took a deep interest in the cause. She really wished that "every parent in town could hear the lectures; they were *so* much needed, and they would do *so* much good." But one day I saw her gliding along to a cupboard, her little boy tripping after. Soon she furtively slipped in her hand, and snatched out a golden and most tempting piece of cake, and slid it into the hand of the child; while she leaned down to his ear with the softly whispered injunction (but I heard it), "There: now go, and do it." And this was a pattern mother of the town. It seemed as if a blow fell on my naked heart. "Ah! how little good am I doing, after all!" thought I. "All is vanity," said the Preacher of old. "All is vanity" was then despairingly echoed by one poor preacher of the present.

Many have a habit of threatening as a means of government. You will hear them say, "I'll put you into the closet," or "out into the entry," or "down cellar!" How seldom is the threat executed! Thus the parent not only betrays an utter powerlessness, but also sets an example of falsehood. But if the offender shall, at length, be thrust into the fearful place, the uncomfortable spirit is not thrust out of him. He scratches, he pushes, he thumps the door; he splits his mother's ears with his screeches for some five long minutes, perhaps; when she, quite overcome, opens a chink just to parley a little, — to say, "Now, my son, if you'll only behave yourself, I'll" — but she does not finish her proposition; for he puts his two hands through that strip of daylight, pushes aside the door, and his mother too, and rushes out like the gust of a tempest. Then he continues to plague that weak-souled parent till weariness and sleep imprison him for the night; yet only to be let loose again in the morning, — the same little storm-spirit as before, ever blowing the parental threat back on the breath that uttered it.

I have known those who would have been perfectly horrified at the idea of a woman's presuming on her right to exercise the butchering business, and to wield the knife and the cleaver, — I have heard such threaten most fiercely to *skin* their own offspring; to skin them alive; to take off every inch, as sure as they were born.

I have heard even more terrible threats than these. One day, as I was passing some Irish dwellings in Boston, my ears were suddenly shocked by the exclamation, in a fierce, feminine voice, together with the native brogue, " If you don't go 'long, I'll kull ye!" I was seized with a curious impulse, and, in a moment, was within the door whence came the screech; and there sat a handsome young Irishwoman, looking not at all as if she really meant to kill her little boy, who, near by, looked not at all as if he expected to be murdered by his own dear mother. I did not soften her surprise at my unexpected intrusion with even a " Good-morning!" but put the question at once, " Do you mean to say that you intend to kill your child?" and she burst out into a good-natured laugh, and replied, " Oh! I have to use the buggest word I can thunk of, or he won't go 'long." As I left this poor, ignorant Irish mother, I could not but reflect that there is also many an American parent, better off in every way, who uses big words to make a child " go along;" and often, the bigger the word, the more he will *not go*.

In these days of humane ameliorations, corporal punishment savors of cruelty, and is by many considered a shocking barbarity. Few parents can bear to have bodily pain inflicted on a child at school; yet I have often seen those who are given to the most excessive indulgence, and who would almost melt with tears of sympathy at any accidental trouble to the darling, — I have seen such, in momentary excitement, assail that same tender creature with a violence which would be deemed entirely behind the age, if resorted to at school. Here is a catalogue of such parental inflictions: pats, slaps, pulls, dabs, twists, twitches, tweaks, pinches, pokes, pushes, cuffs, shakings (almost to very pieces), downright whippings with a little stick, and possibly thumps with something heavier still.

It may, however, really be necessary sometimes to resort to corporal punishment; to give a real, old-fashioned whipping with the old-fashioned rod, — even Solomon's rod. The strong, lower nature cannot be subdued, perhaps, any other way. This is often the case when due discipline has been neglected too long. Sometimes a hardened child or youth comes from unfaithful hands into other and more conscientious care; and it is felt, at length, that decided steps are to be taken. Now, if there is to be whipping, let it be a *whipping*, especially if the subject is of considerable size. Let some time elapse between the offence and the punishment, that the culprit may think the matter over, feel his guiltiness, and shrink from the correcting hand before it is lifted: thus his soul shall be whipped as well as his body, and with more than twofold effect. Then, when the hour of infliction shall come, let it be a solemn hour, — a season of earnest prayer for a right spirit; let it be as if the heavens darkened down, and the guardian angels were looking through the gloom with starry eyes, taking note of the transaction in their books of remembrance, from which you yourself are to be judged. So let it be, and such a punishment may be blessed by the Most Merciful, and be the beginning of a permanent reform.

There are numerous mild methods of discipline which may be adopted with all desirable results in the case of many little offenders. Give a child nothing to do; fasten him to a seat: let there be nothing which he can play with, or any way use, within reach, — not even a particle of sand; for, if there shall be, he will try to solve with it the problem of the infinite divisibility of matter. Restless activity is almost as constant a condition and want of his nature as breathing is. Let him, then, have plenty of the opposite inaction; burden him with nothing to do; and you are about as likely to reach the difficulty as in any other way,— this, too, without absolute bodily pain.

You may send a wrong-doer to bed in the bright daytime. Take away his clothes, and every possible occupation; and then let him continue — rolling from side to side, seeking rest, not to his body, but to his feelings — until he shall resolve to amend, and shall humbly promise so to do. But give not over until you conquer, if it shall take a month. There are various other privations of customary pleasures and comforts which might be tried with good effect. Let there be an inevitable certainty, that any specific transgression shall be punished with some specific privation, and the method, in most cases, will be successful.

Let me not be understood as advising an iron rigor, with its hard, sharp, cutting severity. I simply counsel resolution and efficiency, accompanied by as much mildness as Christian love can breathe into your character. There may be all the firmness of the rock, with all the velvet softness of the mosses that grow upon and adorn it. The child respects real authority. When he knows and feels that the parent possesses a truly conscientious determination, together with all due parental love and tenderness, reverence and love are likely to be his permanent dispositions. To obey, when occasion requires, will be a habit. Take an illustration from the sun: there he stands, — the great paternal luminary, — keeping around him and holding fast his family of worlds, each in its proper place; pouring out his golden beams, awakening the verdure, opening the flowers, ripening the fruits, profusely shedding beauty, but making no *noise*. Let it be so with parentage centred in the home, — strong, loving, luminous, quiet, but ever there; an unmoved, immovable, central power. Why should not children love and grow and blossom and be blessed under such unfailing, genial influence?

Another mode of amendment is to keep a record of failings and amendments. An admonition of to-day is often forgotten by to-morrow, in the whirl of giddy thought. Again: words may be uttered, in reply, not altogether respectful in tone, if they should be in meaning. This may excite harshness in the parent; and then really disrespectful language in rejoinder bursts out from the child, and both advice and authority are more unheeded than ever. All this may be avoided by a silent record in a blank book.

There, in the kindest spirit, explain the nature of a wrong disposition, and put down the several circumstances of any instance of misconduct. Now, this will be a momentous matter to a child. It is in black and white, almost like print. It can be read in solitude, and in moments of sober reflection, when the words of wisdom and tenderness will be apt to sink deep into the heart. This record does not perish in the air like words uttered by the mouth. There it is, to meet the eye again to-morrow, or a month or a year hence. There it is, moreover, to be seen by the other parent,— the father, for instance,— when he shall come in. To a daughter tenderly attached to a father, it is a fearful spectacle, — that of this beloved and revered parent reading such a record with a tearful eye, a saddened countenance, and a meaning glance now and then at the misdoer. Let the child's character, as it unfolds, continue to be registered, the good as well as the evil; the improvements in an especial manner, as an encouragement. If an ordinary story shall be of use, this cannot but be so. It is the child's own passing life and changing character put into a permanent book,— the life giving back visible lessons to the heart from which that life has issued forth.

Finally: one of the surest methods of securing filial reverence and obedience is to surround and consecrate the relation of parent and child by religious associations. Next to that of God, the name of the earthly parent should be hallowed. In the nearest possible relationship stand father and mother to the Father in heaven. They receive the soul from his generating spirit; they take the body from his framing hand. They receive the charge of life directly from the Self-existent and Eternal Life. Who approach nearer to the Lord God Almighty than they? Verily, if any relation is holy, it is theirs. At first, they stand between the Most High and their offspring. They are the shadowing-forth of his power and majesty and love. It is through them that he bows the heavens, and comes down to the least of his little ones on earth. For the child, in the first instance, does not know any thing concerning his heavenly Parent; but he does know his own visible father and mother. These are a sort of first deities to him: they are great, very great, to his littleness. Their might is irresistible, their authority absolute, their care ever ready, their love unfailing. All he possesses and enjoys is chiefly from them. They are the first, the greatest, the wisest, the most affectionate, and the most tenderly beloved beings known. Home, moreover, is all the heaven of which he at first knows. Now, when the idea of the Father most high, our Father in heaven, is presented, the little soul but runs up from inferior attributes, with which he is already acquainted, to higher ones of a similar kind. How important, then, that the earthly relative should most truly show forth the qualities of that relationship which is of all others the highest and the holiest! As the little learner shall associate one with the other, how will the reverence and obedience to both be intermingled and confirmed, and become an abiding and controlling principle of the life! Let that parent, then, be faithful, not so much to his own as to the heavenly Father's child. It is through him as an instrumentality that the Eternal would bestow his earliest and his best blessing on the newly existent immortal, especially the blessing of spiritual and religious nurture. He is consecrated to a holier work than ever was priest, and in a holier temple than was ever reared by human hands. He is to lead this undying spirit to its own Father in the highest, in the temple of home. In this place,

NO-GOVERNMENT IN THE FAMILY. 57

if anywhere below, there should be an altar, and a worship the purest and the most faithful. If any priesthood should never neglect its duty, the priesthood here should never fail. This family shrine should be the holy of holies to the little one there kneeling. It should be the most sacred as well as the dearest spot on earth. As that revered father shall read the Word, and as he shall lift the devout, sincere soul in prayer, leading the circle of loved and linked hearts to the sole Hearer of prayer, how will he increasingly reflect upon the subdued and solemnized child somewhat of the love unspeakable and the light full of glory which fall upon him from above! The earthly relations will be indissolubly associated with the divine ; and this changeful, lower home, with the everlasting, ever-blessed heavens. Now, with other judicious training, how will reverence for rightful authority possess the filial soul! With due fidelity on the part of those charged with the care of the dispositions and the habits, obedience will become a confirmed characteristic. With faithful endeavors, and with God's blessing, the apostolic injunction can hardly fail to be heeded: "Children, obey your parents in the Lord; for this is right." How solemn will seem that commandment of the Ancient of days, given amid the awfulness of Sinai, yet with graciousness and significant promise, "Honor thy father and thy mother"!

Oh that mothers knew their power! It is as spirit and might from God. There is nothing this side of heaven and the angels so strong as a mother's teaching, prompted by a mother's love, and this, blessed by the divine answering of a mother's prayers. I have a most appropriate illustration.

While in the exercise of a missionary ministry in Boston, I was one day hastening along what was considered not only the crookedest, but the filthiest and the wickedest, street in the city. I had been informed, that, in a cellar there, a half-drunken man and his equally drunken wife were selling liquor to make others wholly drunken, if thereby gain might be added to gain. I felt that I must stop a moment to remonstrate. While in the place, there came in a young man, tall, finely formed, and athletic, with a bright and interesting countenance. He leaned his elbow on the bar, as if waiting for the stranger to retire,— probably that he might more freely obtain his dram. I presumed it seemed to him that I had a sort of missionary aspect. I soon addressed him with a kindly greeting, and received a civil reply. I then inquired if his mother were living. In an instant, his cheek was flushed and his eye moistened; and he tremulously replied, "No, sir: my mother has been dead fourteen years." Then, looking him steadily but kindly in the face, I further inquired, "Did your mother teach you to pray, my young friend? Did she teach you religion?" The color deepened on his cheek, and his eyes filled with tears; and in choked accents he stammered out, "O sir! my mother was a good woman: she did teach me to pray; she did teach me religion. I thought I had religion myself, once; but it is all gone now." I immediately stepped up to his side, took him by the arm, and said, "My young friend, this is no place for you. Come, go with me." Then I led him up those creaking, crazy steps as if he had been the veriest child. I conversed with him a few minutes longer while standing on the pavement, and warm tears fell from his eyes upon the cold, red brick; but, being in haste, I took him to an intelligent friend not far off, and asked that he would detain him somehow till I could return and hold further conversation. But I did not see the young man again. He went soon into the country, returning but once, as I understood, to get some necessary articles; and then he entirely disappeared. I know not what became of him from that time onward. But I received a singular, and to me, at that time, a surprising account of him on that very day. I requested a police watchman of that district to accompany me in the evening in a visit to the many cellar haunts in that street, similar to, and perhaps worse than, the one I had entered in the morning. I wanted his protection from danger, or at least insult, as I wished to make some investigations for a moral purpose, which I was set to do by the committee of the association under which I operated. He told me that he was engaged, and that the whole body of the city police were also engaged, on special duty for that evening. "But," said he, "I can tell you of a young man, who, if you can secure his company, will keep you safe; for everybody in the street is afraid of him." To my exceeding surprise, he mentioned the very person whom I had met in the cellar that morning. This young man had before been the ringleader of the riots of the street, the rowdiest of the rowdy,— the very Anak among the strong. When he came swinging his big fist and screeching with his almost wild-beast voice, the stoutest and the bravest stood aside, and let him pass. He had, at length, been put into jail for riot. From this durance he had just come out. He was considerably sobered, probably, as the watchman knew, and intending to be more cautious in his conduct, but still carrying sufficient of his past reputation to make others stand off and keep clear. At this point in his history, I met him in the cellar. I was a perfect stranger. He had no interest in me. He would not have struck me, perhaps; but he might have turned away surlily, or have given me an insolent reply. But no: I spoke two or three words; they seemed to be spiritually electric,— *mother, prayer, religion;* and the strong and the feared one seemed utterly subdued. I took and led him out of that foul drinking den as if he were the smallest boy that could walk; and I committed him, while in tears like a child, to the care of a friend. It was the remembrance of a mother's teaching and prayers that now came over him. Was it not in answer to those prayers that a way was opened through the stone around the heart, so that the waters of contrition gushed forth, cleansing in their course, and preparing for the regenerating spirit of God?

Now, mothers, will you not teach your children to pray? and will you not pray with them? Will you not teach them religion? Fathers, shall these partners in parentage, shall these hearts joined with yours in the most responsible duties, be the only servants of God who shall teach, pray, and be faithful in that holiest of all places, the home?

LECTURE

ON THE

MANAGEMENT OF THE SELFHOOD.

    I. THE RULE FOR IT.
   II. HOW THIS RULE IS NEGLECTED.
  III. HINTS ON ITS OBSERVANCE.

NOTE.

ESPECIAL attention is invited to the introductory pages of the following Lecture. Here is set forth, though very imperfectly, an all-important principle in education ; one which, if made a chief aim in culture and in life, would change earth to a paradise. The more clearly this shall be understood in the outset, the more effective are likely to be the subsequent strictures and suggestions.

The few physiological hints interspersed, though not appertaining to the main subject, presented themselves so readily, that the opportunity was seized for needful service in this much-neglected direction.

The remarks on the forced and untimely activity of the infantile brain are commended to serious consideration. This all-prevalent error should be conversed upon in the household and in the neighborhood, and the law of soundness be rigidly enforced, if parents would save the helpless child from much suffering, and themselves from harassing discomfort.

LECTURE

ON THE

MANAGEMENT OF THE SELFHOOD.

GOD is love. Prompted by this, he is ever exercising all his infinite attributes to bless his creation. As to human beings, however, he cannot bless them in the highest, without their own consent. If husband and wife, parents and children, brothers and sisters, do not lovingly discharge their mutual duties, then that good cannot be given which God has in store. It is only through their own hearts and hands that domestic felicities can reach them. If neighbors interchange no sincere kindnesses, then the best advantages of vicinage are not enjoyed. So throughout the whole great family of our race: man is, from the heart, to bless man, according to nearness and ability and to opportunity in general, or the common Father's bountiful provisions will be unused and his plans not carried out. God must abide by his own wise and pre-existent laws. He will not crush the order of his universe for the sake of those who refuse to conform. Whoever, therefore, does his duty to others, is in his own person, as it were, the lengthening-out of the arm of the Infinite Giver; so that he drops his bounty into capacities otherwise unreached. Whoever does not perform his duty to others, hinders even the Almighty from bestowing the good he intends. Indeed, the Most Merciful is at any moment actually waiting to pour sweet satisfactions through the hearts and lives of millions; but they will not let him. Unloving relatives, quarrelsome or neglectful neighbors, and unjustly warring nations, turn away from the infinite fountain of good, and will not receive its ever-ready streams.

It is a common idea, that the recipient of a favor is the one most benefited; but it is not so, if we consider the inner as well as the outer life. The bestower, if he possesses a right motive and spirit, is more blessed than the receiver. He has the satisfaction of witnessing another's increased enjoyment, and of being the object of thankfulness and of warmer attachment. But it is not necessary to the enjoyment of doing good that the object of it should know whence it comes, so as to be grateful to the individual benefactor. There is a reward richer than the deepest gratitude or the tenderest sensibility of the person benefited: it is that which arises from, indeed which exists *in*, the affection itself that prompts to the action. The love which is not only felt, but which is disinterestedly active, toward another, is the very essence of happiness. The divine and all-perfect character will illustrate this. God is love. The infinitely intense consciousness of this love, the never-ceasing outflowing of it through innumerable channels in his recipient creation, are what constitute his blessedness; at least, in a large degree. It is not what his children feel toward him and do for him that makes him happy, but what he feels toward and does for them. Just so the highest felicity of man consists in the possession, the consciousness, and the outflowing of a similar love. In all the relations of life, it is not what we receive from others which gives us the purest and most intense pleasure: it is what we feel inwardly toward them.

Once, in my own presence, a mother, holding her infant upon her lap, and gazing intently into its face, exclaimed, "Oh! I could sit here all day, and ask for no other happiness than to look at this darling child." She was blessed in her own overflowing maternal heart. It was not in the filial reciprocation of it; for that infant could not yet appreciate and feel in return. It is the same in all the other domestic affections, and likewise in the still wider relationships. It is what each one feels toward another that is the most thrillingly intense, and that makes the most precious part of the heart's treasures. It is not the consciousness of reciprocated attachment, though this truly adds to the happiness.

In the circle of friendship, it is not the attentions shown us, or the presents we receive, which most enhance that circle: it is what we feel toward and do for them. To a properly cultivated and noble nature, there is far more gratification in making a birthday or a New-Year's present than in receiving one.

Again: the benefactor to the poor is blessed in the very consciousness of a benevolent disposition; but he is doubly blessed when this disposition is moved, and gushes out afresh in a new act of kindness. The late Amos Lawrence of Boston gave perhaps of his abundant means from a sense of duty; but he gave also because he *loved* to do it: it made him happy as such things do the angels. When the good doer lets not his left hand know what his right doeth, then no praise of men or no self-praise disturbs the pure thrilling bliss of the prompting, Heaven-like love.

Florence Nightingale left her healthful, rural home in England, and shut herself up in a hospital, in crowded, smoky London, to tend upon poor invalid women. She betook herself to this work, not for money or for distinction, but from that sweet benevolence of the heart which is its own reward. She went to the Crimea, and confronted sickness and death in all its horrors, to relieve the suffering soldier. She made herself so useful and dear to the wretched, that the very shadow of her person falling on his pillow was kissed by him in the impulsive throb of his grateful bosom. All the emoluments the English Government could bestow in compensation, all the honors royalty might vouchsafe, to this noble woman, would have been no inducement to superintend those pestilential hospitals. She went because she loved to go. Her heart carried her thither, and her reward was in the heaven of her own bosom.

Thus we perceive the principal ground on which was given the golden command, "Thou shalt love thy neighbor as thyself." It was because self-forgetful love toward other living beings is the central spirit and inmost life of true and lasting happiness. To love God with all the heart, and the neighbor as one's self, is to receive the very kingdom of Heaven into the heart. It is to receive Jesus Christ and the Holy Spirit and God himself. It is to be like God to the utmost extent in which the finite can approach the Infinite in affection and blessedness.

But how little have mankind understood this philosophy of their nature, and the loving will and beneficent laws of God! Even the majority of those brought up under Christian influences do not understand. They live and act as if happiness was something outside of them, or something to be grasped after, struggled for, and taken in. By each individual's thus feeling and acting, there comes a collision of one person's self with another person's self, and mutual repulse, loss, and disappointment. If any do succeed in gratifying the lower and selfish nature without offence to others, yet how poor and miserable they are notwithstanding!

Each successive generation of mankind educates its offspring in the same ignorance, to make the same mistake, and to suffer the same wretched disappointment. Parents, by their own spirit and example, train and lead their children to shut out that kingdom of God which is waiting to come into their souls in all its fulness and felicity. Even the majority of professedly Christian parents, who really desire better things as far as they are sincere, do, from almost the earliest consciousness of their children, educate them into this unchristian and most unheavenly selfishness. They do that which it seems to me they would utterly abhor; that indeed which all loving and rational parents would abhor, if they did but understand the true philosophy of happiness. Why should they rather curse than bless those who are so dear to their hearts?

I propose now to show some of the occasions and circumstances through which children are educated to dispositions and habits of selfishness.

Human beings, however pure, could hardly but manifest something like selfishness in the very earliest life; because, through utter ignorance and inexperience, they would be conscious only of their own pleasures and pains. Their first attention, in the very nature of things, must be directed to themselves; and, if they should not be specially informed, they must come quite slowly to recognize the welfare of their fellow-creatures. Besides this primary and necessary regard for self, there is very early developed, in innocent ignorance, as human nature now is, an unheavenly self-seeking. Even should there be no injudicious treatment on the part of friends, children in different degrees, according to native constitution, show, quite universally, that they do not love their neighbor as themselves. It requires the most faithful effort and discipline to bring the child to this best law of life. Indeed, it needs the regenerating spirit of God to purify the soul from self-love. Watchful care and training only put the soul in a receptive attitude, that the Holy Spirit may enter, and make way for the fulness of the kingdom of love.

It is of unspeakable importance, at the earliest possible period, to check this inborn, perverse selfishness, and to open the heart to better dispositions. But, as methods generally are, the original tendency is perpetually strengthened. Parents, older brothers and sisters, and other friends, join in the baleful, cruel work of intensifying self; and, of course, multiplying the miseries which must be the consequence.

A first injudicious step is a premature awakening of the intellect. It is very gratifying to parents and others of the family to observe a child's opening faculties, and especially to receive from him an individualizing look. Hence, at the earliest stage, particular effort is made to induce him first to recognize them, and next to notice the inanimate objects around. At length, he does observe more and more, with less and less prompting and direction from others. He now not only sees, but desires to take hold of and to become acquainted with, things. Soon this new intellectual appetite comes to be an urgent want; and, unless it is gratified, the infantile looker is uneasy, and wriggles about: he is sometimes quite uncomfortable, and cries aloud. He must know, and he must *have* too. His mind outruns his bodily ability: so others must go and come and bring for him. If he craves what should be denied, he *must* have it, or he screeches like — not a little innocent child. So the harm must be risked, for he cannot be reasoned with; or, if refusal is absolutely necessary, how prolonged cries of disappointment, and perhaps flashes of temper, pain the parent and trouble the tender-hearted observer! He must not play with fire; he shall not toss and swing about the costly watch as he does his rattle; he may scream, fling out his hands, pucker all up, redden in the face, stretch out stiff, and almost go into spasms, and yet no one can take down for him the new moon or the evening star. Now, I would ask, if it would not be better to leave the child to put forth his mental powers more slowly: and then a *self*, that cannot be gratified without tasking and wearying others, will not be so readily and excessively developed. The grown-up, with their many faculties in the highest state of development, do not desire what they never thought of; and why should the child crave and cry for what he knows nothing at all about? Again: inasmuch as the feeble perceptives easily tire of the same object, a frequent change is demanded, and must be had, or there is no peace. So there is a hurried, and often an anxious, seeking for something new for the unnaturally awakened curiosity. This cannot be put down at will, though the nerves of all concerned painfully suffer.

By such management, the larger portion of infants in civilized society require some one to hold them, to wait on them, to carry them about, and to supply new objects of interest; or, in other words, to amuse them. We now not only have the phrases, "Tend the baby," "Mind the baby," but "*Amuse* the baby." He must have amusements, as a fashionable woman must have parties, balls, and theatres to keep her from being miserable. He has time on his hands to be killed, like some foolish, grown-up people, who have no regular occupation. In this way, at the very earliest, the inborn, selfish tendencies are hurried forth, and hardened into abiding habits. Thus the quite young child becomes the veriest tyrant of the household.

It was not intended that the mind should grow in strength and activity disproportioned to the ability of the material coverings and instruments: as an illustration will make evident. Who would prematurely make a child stand, and bear his weight, on his soft, tender foot, and slender, yielding leg? All know the danger of distorting the little member out of shape. The babe must lie at length, before he can sit; he must roll and sidle along before he can creep; and creep before he can stand or walk. We wait for nature gradually to accumulate strength, sure that this strength will be well used in good time. Other parts of the frame are weak in proportion, — the hand, arm, stomach, and the very organs of speech. However much the infant wonder may think and have to say, he cannot command his organs of speech till they have attained a certain degree of growth, consistency, and strength. The little material organization, in a harmonious and healthy development, is feeble alike throughout. Of course, the brain, being made of matter, is subject to the laws of matter, and is certainly weak with the rest of the body. Ought it, then, to be exercised too early, any more than any other member? Indeed, the brain, in substance, texture, and complexity, is probably one of the most delicate organs of the whole system; and none is more liable to be harmed by premature use. Every act of observation, every newly awakened desire, tasks the brain: every ebullition of passion, — yes, the least emotion of disappointment, — when the flitting wish must be crossed, also tasks the brain. This early rousing of the perceptions by the quickly successive showing of objects, this carrying of the child in some new direction to see things, and this bringing of other things to him to be seen, in consequence of the prematurity, is a similar folly with that by which a child is put too early and assiduously to his school and his books; which course is now considered physically and mentally destructive, and foolish in the extreme.

If, however, the habit of a premature curiosity has been formed, or there is a very peculiar constitution, it will require much reflection and wisdom to deal with it; but, somehow, it ought to be modified and regulated. For health's sake, then, let alone the infant brain, or, more properly speaking, the mind that moves it. Do not permit the intellect to peep through the senses at the strange things of this new earth-scene any faster than need be. When the little observer shall come to carry himself,—first upon creeping toes and knees, and then upon his independent feet,—still permit him to make his discoveries but slowly, and stay as long at each one as will in any wise content him. In this way, you will not stretch and twist and shatter his tender nervous system by premature and excessive action. He will thereby also, at the soonest, begin to form an important intellectual habit,—that of fixed and continued attention. His little perceptives will not be wearied and worn as they would have been if tasked earlier: so that now he can continue longer at an object without weariness or harm; at least, he can take his own abundant time, and not engross the precious hours or minutes of another. By such a holding-back, or rather by this not hurrying forward, how will the comfort, and perhaps health, of others be spared? Ah! that older sister will not be so often kept from pastime or study, or from easier and useful occupation, to tend the babe; tossing him this way and that; reaching up and taking down, first one thing, and then another; again stretching on tiptoe, and, with tip-fingers, getting at still something else for his gratification; or tugging with him backward and forward, shifting from one aching arm to another, and hushing and humming her breath away, to soothe him if he must be disappointed; and, withal, straining her limbs, wrenching her sides, twisting her spine, perhaps crippling her for life, and possibly crushing her into an earlier grave, as has actually been the case with thousands.

Another misfortune may also sometimes be avoided,— that of an ignorant and self-serving domestic stealthily dealing paragoric to stupefy the unquiet little creature into sleep, endangering health, and even life. Thus, by letting alone, and patiently waiting Nature's period, the child is far more likely to retain his precious health and sweet gentleness, and to have a timely ability proportioned to his age. Indeed, from what bodily distemperaments and mental uneasiness at present, and unnumbered ills in future, shall the unconscious innocent be saved! Still further, from what unmelodious cries and painful sympathies and wearisome tendance shall the kindly household likewise escape!

Please not to understand that I would neglect real and absolute wants: these may be more or less numerous and urgent, according to native constitution; and must receive due attention. But I do say,—and I say it with emphasis,—let the soul work its way through the senses without pressure and any hastening effort, just as the flower emerges from the bud. It will be all the more thrifty, symmetrical, and lovely for being left to itself. Nature, whether in her inanimate or animate organizations, must be permitted her own time and methods.

The necessity of food is one of the most frequent occasions for the development of selfishness in one of its basest forms,— that of sensuality.

The human organism, like any other machine, wears out, and needs mending up. Food is the mending substance. In any case of repair, the skilful mechanic applies just enough additional material to remedy the defect, — to make the structure as much like a new one as possible, and no more. The waste made in the animal body is to be supplied precisely according to the same rule, — just as much fresh material, in the form of nutriment, is to be added as will answer the end, and no more. In the case of the child, however, the means of growth, besides this, are to be furnished; or the machine is to be completed, — that is, brought to its full size. The want is indicated by hunger. This ceasing, the Creator's end has been answered. An overplus of aliment would tend to impede the action of the organism, and to disfigure its symmetry. In the repair of a watch, a little too much new material would disturb the delicate mechanism, and the needed exactness of movement would be lost. Further and clumsier tinkerings would stop it dead. Is it not the same with this human timepiece, which ticks the moments with heart-beats? God's law of mechanical proportions and adjustments, in the case of his living workmanship, is temperance; and this law cannot be violated with impunity. Yet, alas! how continually is it transgressed! In this land of plenty and indulgence, many children eat quite as much for pastime and mere sensual pleasure as for use. Simple, nutritious food, Nature's best mending stuff, will not suffice, as the relish for such depends on Nature's healthy appetite. Artificial tastes are excited by artificial luxuries, and these soon become pressing wants. How does the evil begin? Just to amuse the newly weaned, or perhaps the unweaned, infant; just to amuse,— nothing more is intended,— a crum or a spoon's-tip of some rich compound is put to his mouth. The flavor is now first experienced; and the little creature, whose frame the Creator would build strongly up from the purest elements, is thus initiated into high living. A little further on in his months, he troubles the busy housekeeper: so some dainty diverts attention while she accomplishes her affairs. Or some tired attendant, in this way, relieves herself from his uncomfortable humors. Well, a taste is fairly formed for eating: eating becomes a fastened habit. It is one of the ways in which a smart little fellow, two years old, kills time. He is really dissipated. At peep of day, he gives his mother a slap, or his father a push, or the nurse (if she has the care) a pinch, and wants cake, pie, candy, or some other good thing. Then, all day long, there must still be, besides the family meals, an occasional tribute to the palate. He is dull and uncomfortable: he wants amusement; so he amuses himself with eating, as some other time-killers do with drinking. As they whet up the appetite for dinner, or more probably, in the long-run, blunt it down, by gin, brandy, or rum; so this little beginner prepares himself for the meal by a spicy piece of mince-pie or an unctuous doughnut. He thus early becomes a gross voluptuary.

What, now, is the consequence? In the earlier stages of this gluttonous career, thousands and thousands are borne to the grave, indirectly killed by sheer indulgence. Accidental colds are made worse, and promoted to violent fevers; disorders of the bowels are engendered; hereditary diseases, like the scrofula, more easily fasten an incurable hold; indeed, ills untold and unimagined are brought upon the weak and overloaded system. According to reliable statistics, about one-quarter of all that are born die under five years of age. Of course, how much larger the number driven from the stage of life between birth and the adult period! No doubt, impure air and various other circumstances are partly the cause; but this premature destruction might yet be very much diminished by fitness, temperance, and regularity in diet.

Ah! could parents but once clearly understand how fearful as well as wonderful is this organism of muscles, fibres, nerves, tubes, and infinitesimal ducts, together with the speeding currents, oozing juices, and dew-like distillations; and how they twist and clog and mat and mash them up by their blind, their almost insane, indulgence, — methinks they would fall on their knees, and lift hands and eyes and voices to the Author of life, supplicating pardon for the murderous past, and wisdom and firmness for the future; and thus this terrible havoc of the innocents would be abated.

In our abundant country, people of the most ordinary means might take a lesson, in this matter of eating, from the nobility of England. It is said, that all along up through childhood certainly, and somewhat into youth, their children are not permitted those luxuries which load the daily table for the gratification of their elders. By such judicious restraints, as well as by other circumstances, this class of people is insured that degree of robust health for which it is so distinguished. Indeed, we might take a further lesson from even regal families. Victoria, it is said, exhibits a truly queenly wisdom in the education of the royal heirs. No doubt, that, in her family, sound dietetic rules are observed as well as other important principles of discipline. The husband and father, it is well known, co-operates with the most conscientious faithfulness, and lends a strong, steady, governing hand.

It may be stated, in addition, that the children of the Russian czars are altogether unaccustomed to harmful luxuries. The dietetic laws appertaining to them are absolute. In this manner must the present autocrat have been educated. Thus he has inherited, and continues to enjoy, a sound body to go with that sound intellect and great heart which bestows freedom, as well as commands obedience, among the sixty millions of his vast empire. If every citizen sovereign in our country would train his children with a similar inflexible wisdom, what a robust, healthy, and truly majestic potentate should we at length become, seated in million-fold unity on our august continental throne!

But the moral effect is far worse than the physical. In the first place, the temper is injured. The overloaded and distended system causes frequent uncomfortableness, and sometimes severe pain: thus the naturally mild of disposition become sensitive and irritable, and the constitutionally irascible are more readily developed into as fiery imps as unwise parents need be tortured and punished by. In this way is started the selfishness of a vindictive spirit, which, in the distant future, may flame forth in deeds of cruelty and destruction. A base nettle is cherished which pierces everybody that touches it, and whose prickles will be blown by occasional gusts of passion against all that come near.

But this eating propensity is, in itself, a selfishness still lower down than the temper which it occasions; and it is the broad stair, next to the steep descent, to more dangerous intemperance and to viler lust. It prepares the young to be more excessively dissipated after leaving the restraints and the oversight of home. Our large cities are thronged with young men who are at one stage or another of sensualism. Some are sinking down to the lowest dissoluteness. Look into certain places on an evening, and there they are, indulging the depraved appetite; not only eating the dainties which simple nature does not crave, but drenching and scorching nature with liquid fire; becoming, it may be, inebriates for life. Whence did they come?

Who are they? Sons of the farmers, of the mechanics, of the traders, of the lawyers, of the doctors, of the legislators, and perhaps of the judges and governors, of the land. Ah me! — must the humiliating confession be made? — some of them are quite likely to be the sons of the ministers of our churches. In many cases, these youths have been led to the brink of the gulfs of ruin by their own parents at home. They have been trained to think of and live for the palate. A city merchant informed me, that out of thirty acquaintances of his youth, clerks in neighboring stores, one-half died in early life of dissipation, and some of them were connected with the most respectable families of the State.

One sabbath forenoon, while speaking in a country church on the temptations and dangers of city life, I observed a young man sitting uneasily, and coloring in the face. He absented himself from the afternoon service. He declared, as I was told, that he wouldn't go to meeting to hear a minister talk in that sort of way. He was then on a visit from Boston to his relatives. Within four weeks from that time, his corpse was brought from the city, and cast, dust to dust, near the church where he had so lately sat, angry at the preacher's truth. He had died of disease brought on by dissipation. Now, had these ruined youths been trained to the true uses of food, to a conscientious temperance, from infancy up, how different, probably, would have been their fates! How would they have blessed the restraining prudence of their parents through prolonged and healthy years!

Apparel is another bodily want; and it is the occasion of an unheavenly selfishness in the form of vanity. Vanity says, "Don't look at him or her, but behold me!" An early disposition is the love of finery, and the attention it attracts. The child hastens to exhibit some new article of attire or ornament. There may be a quite innocent pleasure in possessing it, and a wish for sympathy; but, withal, there is likely to be an unamiable vanity. A little girl, some three years old, wore for the first time, in church, a dress with a pocket. She whispered, "Mother, do you think that Mr. ——" (naming the minister) "knows that I have a pocket in my dress?" There was here an incipient vanity which might grow to be monstrous. That child, left unchecked, coming to be the miss of sixteen, might trip and mince to church, with her fashions and her attractions uppermost in her mind.

But no wonder that this vice should so banefully blossom out, when parents themselves so often nurture it from the earliest. To gratify their own vanity, how they bedeck the darling, and even overload with finery! Some children seem like huge insects of the summer,—very aristocrats of the gaudy and gauzy tribes; and, to use a phrase which will be understood, fit to be the "big-bugs" of the naturalist's cabinet. When this vice first shows itself, teach the true uses of apparel. If need be, take off and put away the new, and replace the old, till the desire for display shall be corrected.

There is, however, no objection to the use of the beautiful in the attire of children; but there must be adaptation to the age, or the beautiful will not be there, or at least its charm will have fled. How admirable is Nature in her simple flower-buds! She reserves her large and far-seen fashions for the full, expanded bloom. Cannot parents apply this example, divinely ordained, to the living, priceless blossoms of their own households?

Next, there are house, furniture, and style of living, as an occasion, not only of vanity, but of pride. It is by no means intended to disparage well-gotten wealth, and the elegance it affords. The eye was formed to be pleased. The Almighty designed and made things to please it. The tasteful arts are but the faint imitations of his own works. It is only the bad spirit which accompanies possessions and privileges that is to be censured and deprecated.

At a school recess, a little bit of pretension puffs itself up, and exclaims, " Your father isn't as rich as my father is; you don't live in so nice a house as I do." Who instilled such miserable folly into the heart of a child, if not the parents or other inmates of home? Certain young ladies will not notice certain other ones in the street, though they are school companions, belong to the same class in recitation, and are of equally proper manners, and perhaps of more refined character, because, forsooth, the fathers of these latter live in inferior style, and move in a different circle. Now, millions of wealth, the loftiest ancestry, and the most splendid fashion, cannot make such souls lovely or beloved, or truly happy. If death snatch their spirits from the corrupt but cherished flesh, can they be received among those heavenly ones who have been exalted in proportion to their humbleness, and are thought of and loved by others in proportion as they have forgotten themselves? O cruel, cruel parents, with your own trusted breath to puff up the tender, elastic soul into such swollen and repulsive deformity as pride!

Very many of the "first people," as they are called, possess their privileges, it is hoped, without pride. Indeed, there are those whose lack of pretension, whose very humility, might give lessons to all ranks beneath them. Here is an admirable example with which to close this topic. A gentleman of large inherited wealth, and of the best education and culture the country could afford, had two daughters at a school, conducted, not by an ambitious and showy, but by a most thoroughly educated and judicious teacher. The daughter of another gentleman, of limited means and quite economical living,— a bank or insurance clerk, perhaps, — was also an attendant; but she was one of the best scholars in her class, of refined manners and amiable disposition. The two young ladies, on acquaintance with this schoolmate, seemed particularly pleased with her, and made her a special associate at recesses. The circumstance excited attention and surprise. Those of similar position and pretensions with the young ladies ventured to inquire and remonstrate about the matter. "Why are you so intimate with this person?" said they. "Why do you so lower yourselves? Her father's position in life is entirely different from that of yours, and his daughter can never move in the circle that you will." The reply was modestly made: "She is certainly equal to any one of the school in talent and character; and we know no reason why we should not associate and be intimate with her, if we like her, as we happen to do." At length, the father of these young ladies came to the teacher, and made especial inquiries concerning the character of this favorite companion. Perhaps it had been hinted to him by meddlers, that his daughters were forming low associations. He, however, received the most satisfactory assurances from the teacher: so the intimacy continued uninterrupted. When the long summer vacation arrived, this noble-souled father, this thorough Christian gentleman, invited his daughters' friend to spend the leisure weeks at his magnificent country seat, and gave her the opportunity of the best privileges of his own social life. He made no such invitation to those who thought it a degradation to be intimate with the excellent person whose parentage was altogether respectable, but whose rank the world had put a few notches lower, for no other reason than the lack of money and the position it affords.

Education itself, that precious privilege, is made the occasion of developing the most intense selfishness. The prevalent stimulus to study is selfish emulation: higher place in the class, the medal or the book-prize, or other outward honors of scholarship, become the aim. Thus the true end of education is forgotten. No wonder that forceful, fierce ambition should so often manifest itself in after-life, or that political aspiration and demagogism should possess many an otherwise noble soul with a very madness. If love, self-forgetfulness, and humility make heaven, how can this fiery emulation and its bitter heart-burnings, and such worldly towering-up, prepare for the sublime lowliness of heaven?

Here the remark may come in, that parents often make the acquirements of their children the occasion for displaying their own fond conceit, and, in doing so, set a harmful example to the child. You will scarcely have taken your seat in some houses, and have begun to speak of the children, before little Admirable must run and get his book, and show the gentleman how well he can read. Thus the visitor is compelled to witness the exploits of a poor little fellow at stammering and miscalling words; and, withal, his remarkable dexterity at showing how mistaken his doting parent is.

After this early development of self, in connection with the goods of life, the evil cannot but put itself forth to the utmost in the acquisition of them. As these things and all other property are represented by money, the grasping soul is concentrated upon this. Money in due degree, for good ends and by just means, is, of course, a proper object of pursuit; but how has the true idea of it been perverted! Good and use are at length overlooked, and a new passion, a new vice, has taken possession, — the love of money, as money; and how early it appears! The child hardly old enough to articulate gloats over his bits of coin. Even the best affections are transmuted into this money-passion. A boy spontaneously performs a trivial service (perhaps picks up your dropped handkerchief, and restores it), and you as spontaneously offer him a piece of change. How he snatches it, and scuds away to his parents! and how in spirit they snatch it too, in sympathy with his good fortune!

The true reward for a favor is, first, the sweet, loving impulse to do it, and then the agreeable consciousness of having done some little good. Every opportunity to render service to another is a God-send to the little heart. It opens that heart, and fits it for a larger sphere of good-doing at a maturer age. If a reward for such spontaneous favors be received, pure generosity is stifled, and the sordid motive of doing good for pay takes its place.

I have, in my own personal experience, a most charming and impressive illustration of an opposite character, which I cannot forbear to bring in here from a volume where it is in print.

"Early one summer morning, I was travelling in a chaise through this mountain-town.* I had arrived near the outskirts, when I fancied that I heard a singular noise; but did not then stop or look out to see what it might be, as I was in particular haste to reach my destination. I drove rapidly on. But soon the noise again startled my ear, and seemingly the shrill scream of a human being. Still driving on, I leaned out of the vehicle to learn whence came the piercing

---

* Dublin, N.H., on the north side of the Monadnock.

sound. I then discovered a boy pursuing me at the top of his speed, and crying after me to stop; which I now did. He came up nearly exhausted by half a mile's run, with his bosom all open, and his face all reddened with the heat, and reeking with perspiration; and he pantingly exclaimed, 'You are losing your trunk, sir!' At this information, I leaped out; and surely my trunk was in a deplorable condition. It had been fastened beneath the axle-tree. But one of the straps had got broken, and it was dangling by the other, now almost wrested off, having been knocked against the stones, and dragged through dust and mud, till it was a sorry sight. I requested my benevolent informer to stand at the horse's head till I should put it into safety. Of course, such a boy, or any boy, could not but do this under such circumstances. When ready to start again, I held out, in spontaneous gratitude, a piece of money, of more tempting value than our smallest silver coin; and, lo! the little fellow drew back and straightened up, and with a keener eye, and almost an offended tone, exclaimed, '*Do you think I would take pay for that?*' I could not prevail on him to receive the least compensation. I went on my journey, rejoicing in the accident, although it was to cost me the repairing of my torn and bruised trunk. It had made known to me one *magnanimous boy*. For how many much slighter favors had I received from the young, who capered away, insensible to the pleasure of doing a kindness, in the satisfaction of 'taking pay for that'! 'Ay,' thought I, 'this boy is an honor to the common school; he is a Christian learner in my friend the minister's Sunday school; he is a diligent reader of the juvenile library. Blessed pupil of a blessed pastor! thy getting is the true and the best one, — that of understanding: to thee, wisdom is "the principal thing."' How many, many times since have I thought of that boy, and wished that I knew his name, and could trace his onward course! How many times, in my wanderings and stoppings within sight, even within the most distant glimpses of the peaked crown of that proud old hill-king, have I thought of that grand, that royal-spirited boy! That mountain, by natural association, is to me a most fit monument to one magnanimity towering above many meannesses. Ye boys, and indeed ye men, of our country, to whom the moral of my story may apply, I pray you, when you shall perform a little favor spontaneously, or even by request, let your souls stand up in true nobility, in the heavenward grandeur of disinterestedness, and say in the spirit, 'Do you think I would take pay for that?'"*

The manifestations of self, through cunning, duplicity, and positive acts of deception, easily come along after meanness. For instance, a boy swaps knives or pencils with another lad, and then boasts, with a sparkling eye and a chuckling voice, that he has got the best end of the bargain! His parents, it may be, brighten and chuckle too at the early shrewdness and promising thrift; and thus encourage and spur him on. Now, this getting of the best end of the bargain knowingly, and through the unsuspecting ignorance of the other party, is a violation of the golden rule, "to do as we would be done by." It is worse: it is the breaking of the commandment, "Thou shalt not steal;" for it is taking by stealth that for which there is given no equivalent. It is absolute theft in the eye

---

* The people of the town, on seeing the incident in a publication, were curious to know who the young hero might be. After several years, his name was discovered. He proved to be a poor boy who "lived out" at a farmer's to work for his living. His acquaintances at once exclaimed, "Well, it is just like him!" Brief, simple, but most expressive eulogium,—"It is just like him!"

of that Infinite Justice which gave the law on Sinai. The "best end of the bargain" is the worst end of it. Such a beginning of business may lead, at length, either to some great theft or enormous forgery, and to the State Prison. It may prepare the way for grand peculations from government, or for magnificent embezzlements from bank and railroad corporations, and all their infamous glory.

Many forms of injustice prevail in the business world, of which human law takes no cognizance, but which are nevertheless violations of the divine law. The young, almost universally, are educated into this injustice. Children are trained by the example of parents, and indeed by prevalent practice, to a cool, keen selfishness, and habitual unfairness in trade, in the following way: Articles on sale are of a certain specific value when viewed in the relation of cost and of other values, and they ought to command a certain price; but how many are never willing to give a just price! They want the thing for a little less. Suppose a retail store. "Come, now: won't you fall a little? You can afford to take a cent less,—*only* a cent." Sometimes even the half-cent is higgled for. Now, this half-cent is no more for the purchaser to give than it is for the seller to lose; and, in the long-run, it is the half-cents, more or less, on yards and pounds of goods, which make up much of the trader's gains or losses. Thus such people clip off, and press down and screw harder and harder, until they often drive the dealer himself to questionable expedients, in order to make his absolutely necessary profits. By such a spirit and example, children are educated not only to a littleness which is disgusting, but to a wrong which is abhorrent.

Inculcate on the young, by precept and practice, the righteous rule of business, — "to live, and let live;" or rather the great commandment of justice, — " Whatsoever ye would that men should do to you, do ye even so to them." One may claim of a seller a good article; but, then, let him claim, in turn, its full value, and get it — of your son or daughter. "Ah!" replies selfishness, in the guise of suspicion and caution, " in this way the buyer will lay himself open to be continually cheated and wronged." By no means. Justice, candor, and kindness, on his part, will be his best protection. Let a character for uprightness and liberality be once established with a dealer, and, in nine cases out of ten, he would put himself to inconvenience, or even to loss, sooner than occasion inconvenience and loss to such a customer. He would abhor — at least, in good nature, he would disdain — to commit on him a fraud. Meanness is generally its own punishment. It provokes retaliation, and, somehow, gets "come up with" sooner or later.

A somewhat ludicrous anecdote will illustrate this point. A customer at a country store, having supplied his wants, inquired, as it was near the new year, for the next almanac. The trader handed him the indispensable work. The price was asked. "Six cents," was the reply. "Oh! it is too much," the customer rejoined: "I can't give that." — "Very well," said the trader; and, stooping down, he brought from some by-place another copy, with the observation, "Here is an almanac you may have for five cents." The customer, much pleased, paid the money, and took the article. In a day or two he returned to the store, with his purchase in hand, and, much excited, exclaimed, "Sir, you cheated me in this almanac. Why, there are only ten months in it: the other two are torn out!" — "I knew that," replied the trader, very quietly, yet significantly; "but you got all you paid for."

An equally instructive incident comes from another experience: —

"I had been accustomed," said a gentleman, "to purchase my grocery necessaries of a particular trader in our village. One of my neighbors, on a time, hearing me mention the place of supply, exclaimed, " Oh! don't go there: you will certainly get cheated; for I don't succeed well at all with the man." I could not but think in my own mind, that the grocer also, on his part, failed to succeed well with my neighbor; for my experience had been of quite a different kind. On one occasion, at the close of the year, we had a settlement of accounts, and squared up, as had been our custom. The trader then opened a new page, at the head of which he put my name; but he wrote also what he had not written before,— *Hon.* before it. 'What do you mean by that?' said I. 'I have never held any office which gives me a claim to such a title.'—'No matter,' said the trader: 'you *are* honorable; and I have put it down on this account-book, and here it shall stay.'" This gentleman's experience is suggestive to the parental educator. For myself, I should certainly prefer that a son should gain the reputation, and win the unsolicited, unthought-of title, *honorable*, on account of his perfectly just dealing with his fellow-men, than to climb like a reptile, or rush like a vulture, to the highest office of a State, or even to the chief magistracy of the nation.

Early home-circumstances, considered altogether trifling, are the tiny roots of a monstrous growth of immoralities in the future business-life. There are deceptions, trickish annoyances, and various unrebuked, at least unamended wrongs, between children themselves. There are falsehoods and artifices exercised toward parents. These, if discovered, are too lightly passed over. They are not brought into solemn judgment before the religion of Christ and the will of God. But worse: what evasions and subterfuges, prevarications and deceits, in social life, are often practised by parents themselves in the presence of their children! Then what stratagem and double-dealing to manage the children on trying occasions! How often are positive refusals not adhered to, but are melted away by pertinacious teasing! Again: what threats which are never executed! what promises which are never performed! Alas! no wonder that human nature is so often, so early, and so effectually initiated into a life of heartlessness, lying, dishonesty, and dishonor.

I have thus exhibited some of the occasions and circumstances through which children develop dispositions and form habits of selfishness; and, in connection, have given a few impressive contrasts. I would now present some examples of an opposite kind of training. First, then, as you believe in Christianity and in the heaven it reveals, teach a child, as early as possible, to forget himself; to do, and indeed to live, for others. As soon as he shall be able, let him pass with his little hand some needed article to another, and he shall have begun a life of beneficent industry. As soon as he can creep, let him go errands on all fours,— for instance, to carry some manageable thing, perhaps the newspaper, pinned to his clothing, to a person across the room, wanting it; and he shall have possibly begun his journey across the continent, to carry civilization into some new territory; or, as a missionary, to set up the cross of Christianity among the far Heathen, and to give himself up a living sacrifice at its foot.

Train a child to work, not by cold and stern compulsion or merely by the inducements of activity, but for the sake of being of service, of doing some little good. If there are no servants in a family, there are numberless things in which boys and girls can be useful. Beautiful are their dispositions, blessed their lives, if they shall be affectionately helpful. There are thousands of wives and mothers, broken down by hard work and the various burdens of life: not only daughters, but sons also, should aid in making those burdens lighter. In the absence of daughters, things ordinarily done by them could be, and ought to be, done by sons. It is a mere notion, that this and that is girls' work; and that, therefore, it is beneath *boy* dignity to touch it. Whatever is of use is honorable; especially if, through the performance, kind affections flow out. It adds to the dignity rather than detracts from it. He who, whether boy or man, shall honor his father and mother by doing them kind service, most particularly honors himself.

Again: train up a child to such a pursuit as will add to human enjoyment beyond the person's own self. As the chief motive to such a pursuit, let not self-interest, but usefulness to others, be presented. When an apprenticeship, or preparation for business-life, is entered on by a youth, the idea should be strongly inculcated, and thoroughly wrought into the soul, that the avocation is designed by an all-embracing Providence, not so much to enrich and elevate himself, as it is that he may be of use to his brethren of the human race, equally God's children with himself. If one is industrious and prudent, self will be sufficiently taken care of at any rate. The all-loving Father's object is to develop, through certain uses, that love for our fellow-beings which not only makes the truest felicity, but which turns all the energies of the man, and all his external and internal possessions, to the best possible account. To forget self, and to love others, is to be like Divine Perfection: not only so, but to *work* is to be like the Divine. The Deity is the Infinite Worker. If he is the Almighty Master of the universe, he is also the Universal Servant: he ministers to the minutest wants of all. Indeed, it is only through the multitudinous, the innumerable workings of his power, that his love is made known. So far as a human being is idle and useless, so far has he removed himself from the image and likeness in which he was made, and from the felicities that belong to his nature.

The young man who does nothing but saunter about town, and while away his time in trivial conversation or on superficial literature; or the young woman who takes her daily promenade for mere show, who makes her calls for cold etiquette or frivolous gossip, and wastes the rest of her time on the last new novel and in the current amusements, — is a sort of moral monster. The very God who made them is every moment teaching them a lesson of industry; for he tends their very heart-beatings by his own active and ever-present energies. If he stop his work in their idle bodies, they die.

Again: I would train up the young with such dispositions to usefulness, that the desire for it should never cease while life and energy continue. I honor the old merchant who still sticks to his business, and makes his accumulations to the very last, if he only does it, not for the love of money, but for the adding of means to means that he may do good, and communicate abroad.

The very idiot who has a heart to feel for human want and suffering, and has willing hands to relieve according to his ability, is a thousand-fold more to be respected than the man who lives for nothing but to reach out after money; who grasps all he in any way can, and then holds it all close to himself; thinking of it as a possession of his own, and not as a means of usefulness to others.

Many years ago, I resided in a most excellent family, a member of which was a weak-minded boy, eight or ten years of age. He could hardly put together words enough to make a single full sentence, he was so defective in ideas, or at least in speech. Indeed, he could not pronounce his own name; which was Francis. So he called himself by the more convenient monosyllable, "Boy." But he had a most gentle nature; a large and abounding heart, flowing out most sweetly to all around him. Many years sped away, and I hardly knew how they sped with the tenderly remembered Francis. At length, meeting a relative, I made inquiry after him. The reply was, that he had for a long time been at board in an excellent home; that, though a man in stature and twenty-six years of age, he could read no better and could speak no better than when I knew him as a child. Indeed, he could not yet utter his own name, but still, in referring to himself, said "Boy." "But," continued my informant, "he is, though an idiot, *good;* he is kind; he is very loving. It is a great pleasure to him to be taken on occasional visits to the alms-house of the town; and there he makes such presents to the poor inmates as suits his benevolent fancy."

The lady mentioned an incident of recent occurrence, which to me was peculiarly touching; and for the sake of which, as a special illustration, I have now brought this person to notice. "In the course of last winter," said she, "an old man, who lived alone with his wife in the neighborhood, died. Soon after the burial, some women, in the presence of Francis, were conversing on the subject of the old man's departure, and the lonely situation of the widow. Among other things, they wondered who now would cut and split and carry in the poor woman's wood. Immediately Francis was heard to exclaim, 'Boy knows.' His words, however, excited at the time no attention. At length, it was remarked by the neighbors, that Francis every day, regularly, made a visit to the widow's. The people began to be curious, so invariable, and in all weathers, was his going to the house. Inquiry was made; and it was found that he went to cut and split and carry in the widow's wood." Thus, while these neighbors were *wondering who* would do it, and while their own sons should have thought to do it,—indeed, should have been so trained by them as to have rejoiced to do it, — the blessed charity was performed by Francis, the idiot.

When the Framer of bodies and the Father of spirits shall deliver that beautiful soul from its clayey bondage, how will it soar up and up to the region of celestial affection, unspeakably above those who know, but who, with their competent strength, *do* not; who possess, but who of their overflowing abundance *give* not!

If the young shall be rightly trained in the home, and especially if this training is seconded by the Sunday school, they shall begin even in childhood to do, according to a child's measure and means, what they shall perform in their opulent age with a wide-sweeping and a most bountifully dropping hand. The trifling contributions of children, a single cent or a half-dime, on each occasion, will, if heart and wealth shall grow together, become in the distant future the hundred-dollar donation, or the thousand-dollar bestowment in some grand philanthropy; or, it may be, the hundred-thousand-dollar legacy to some noble institution; and this not for show, not for the world's praise, but from that humble, hearty love of doing good which is its own blessing and richest reward, whether the world knows and praises it or not.

Again: it is in the home, and under true Christian nurture, that the missionaries of the cross to Heathen lands are best prepared. Suppose a child trained to read God's word, to learn concerning his heavenly Father therefrom, and the beautiful happy home of many mansions prepared in heaven for his earthly children. Let him be opportunely informed that millions of human beings in other parts of the world are without the knowledge of this dear, loving Father, and have no idea of this pure and blessed home, — are utterly ignorant of that Saviour Son who came into the world to deliver from ignorance and sin all who might hear of and follow him: that child might be so impressed as to melt with pity toward those benighted worshippers of stone and wood, who are so utterly without the true God in the world. With such appliances as a noble Christian mother could make to the little heart, how might he be formed to be another Judson, from the earliest dew upon his life's bloom, and at length bear fruits for the feeding of multitudes in distant lands!

I knew of such a mother. The following circumstances occurred in one of the interior cities of Massachusetts, where I once, for a short time, resided. The example will plead for a true Christian education far better than any theories or the most eloquent setting of them forth. Two little boys had been told by their religiously faithful mother of the destitution of the Heathen as to Christian privileges; especially of their having had no Bible, — that book which the children loved so well to read, and from which they were so constantly and interestedly taught concerning the heavenly Father, and that Jesus who took little children in his arms and blessed them. So it came into their compassionate hearts to give such little moneys as they might occasionally obtain to the Bible Society, of which their mother informed them; thus doing some little part in sending the good book to the Heathen. Of course, they could hardly comprehend the full scope and meaning of such an enterprise; but they had knowledge sufficient to light the way to their continually growing hearts. At length, there was established in that city an Orphan Asylum, where children who were without parents, or who, through intemperate fathers, were perhaps worse off, might have a comfortable home for a time. Somehow, the little boys' sympathies became deeply interested in this institution. Perhaps it was because they could see with their own pitying eyes the wretched sufferers in the street who needed just such a refuge. So, with their mother's consent, the bits of money which they had been accustomed to drop, as they could get them, into the aperture of their tight box for the Bible cause, were now devoted to the use of the Orphan Asylum.

But at length the Lord wanted these children, and took them to himself. They were, I think, smitten with some epidemic, and died within two weeks of each other, respectively, at five and three years of age. Their own special contribution-box was then opened, and the sum of two dollars found, which had fallen from their little hands, and been devoted to the Orphans' Home. Beautiful, inviting, blessed examples of parental training to benevolence and philanthropy! Oh, could the millions of children in our plentiful and privileged country be so educated, how would a thousand, where there is now one, go forth to civilize, to Christianize, the Heathen world!—and how would hundreds of thousands, who at the same time accumulate means by prosperous industry, shed their moneys like sunshine and shower-drops to aid them in making the wilderness glad, and the desert blossom as the rose!

I have something more to add about the elder of the two boys. It was remarkable how he exhibited the ruling passion, if we may so call it, if not in death, at least in sickness, and as long as he well could. In the commencement of his disease, although compelled to stay at home from school, he was yet well enough to range the house. But how marked the contrast between his method of amusement or his child-work and that of the majority of children who might be kept in similar durance! He put his school-books into his little satchel, and imagined himself a colporter carrying good Christian books to the destitute inhabitants of the newly settled West, in imitation of modes of action which he had read of in the religious papers, or heard about from his parents or at the Sunday school. As if going from house to house, he would knock at the door of a room; then, as if hearing an expected voice, enter, and make his salutations to the imaginary inmates, courteously inquiring if they would like to take some good books which had been sent by some excellent people for their use. Thus he proceeded from room to room in this beautiful, evangelic play, until the very moment, for aught I know, when he was cast upon that bed from which he arose, in his spirit-form, to meet the welcoming angels.

The Son of God bows himself down from the right hand of the infinite throne to bless such children, and to breathe on them his Spirit. Parent, he would thus do to your own little ones: he only waits for you to bring them nearer to the heavenly courts.

PASSAGES FROM A LECTURE.

I. — GIFTS.

IT is customary in many families, perhaps in most of any considerable culture, to interchange gifts, especially on the usual annual occasions. This is well. By these tokens, the affections are drawn out, interwoven, and bound fast. But it should be understood, that it is not so important for the parent to bestow on the child, as for the child to bestow on the parent. Filial love is enhanced far more by *giving* than by receiving. In this there is something much better than accepting, and being grateful. The affectionate heart must prompt, the excited intellect must contrive, and the diligent hand must execute. There must be a series, perhaps a long series, of impulses, thoughts, and actions. All these have reference to the beloved relative, and they all develop the heart more and more toward him. The more numerous the antecedents to the bestowment, the more developed is the love which prompts the beautiful attention. I have a true story charmingly appropriate to the subject: —

The celebrated Scotch phrenologist, Mr. George Combe, when travelling on the continent of Europe, fell in with a distinguished musician as a fellow-passenger in a stage-coach. The artist remarked to him, while speaking of his profession, that he had a son who was as accomplished a performer as himself on the violin, his favorite instrument. "I discovered," said he, "that he had a remarkable talent for music when he was about six years of age. On one of my birthday mornings, I was awakened from sleep, at break of day, by hearing my favorite tune performed on my favorite instrument most enchantingly. In delightful amazement, I tossed away the clothes, and looked out; and what did I behold? — my darling boy thus making a birthday present to his father.

"I found, on explanation, that, months before, he had obtained the instrument from his mother, together with her consent to his little plan: so he practised that one tune particularly and continually, till he had perfected himself in it. Then, when the day came and the dawn first gleamed, he stole to his father's bedside, and poured his birthday present into his ear.

"And what did you do, sir?" inquired Mr. Combe.

"I wept."

II. — BAD COMPANIONSHIP.

PARENTS often complain of the bad companionship to which their children are exposed. "If our boys," say they, "could only have proper companions, it would be easy enough to manage them; and all would go right." To such complainers, let it be said that there is one method of securing good companionship, which is not sufficiently thought of. Let parents themselves be companions to their sons and daughters, and the best of companions too. The public-house or the village-store is no place for a father's leisure time. Home is his proper place; his family, his richest possession: and training and making happy his children, his appointed and his highest work. It should be his most delightful work. Let not his private reading absorb all his time, while the children cower stilly in the corner, or run riot without disturbing his abstractedness. Let him join them at times in their juvenile literature, sympathize with them in its entertainments, and aid them to apply its instructions. Indeed, the little golden cups of genius, proffered now by many eminent writers, cannot but refresh and nurture even the adult mind.

Again, let the father — let both parents condescend to mingle in the children's pastimes, and they will enjoy such playfellows full as well as those of their own age. Ever let them remember, however, to leave their play without having lost any of the strength or the dignity of parentage.

A highly respected merchant, speaking of his own methods of discipline, remarked that he never had the least difficulty from his children's wandering off with bad companions, or wishing to wander. "We take care," said he, "frequently to invite, for an evening, virtuous and most unexceptionable young acquaintances to our house. We join most heartily in the juvenile sports. Indeed we task our own minds to invent new games for our mutual recreation; and truly we do succeed in making home the happiest place in all the world to our children."

Another gentleman, careful as to the exposure of his sons, adopts especial means to keep them from bad associations on holiday occasions. For instance: if there is to be no great public celebration on a Fourth of July in his little city, and yet the population are all loose abroad, he would keep his own sons at home. So he gets up a celebration of Independence within his own domestic domain. He prepares, in connection with his children, a regular programme of exercises. He constitutes himself the president of the day, and makes an oration. Then the whole family contrive to get up toasts. One son is a toastmaster; and another son writes an ode, as he is something of a poet. The whole celebration is concluded by a few fireworks in the yard. In the mean time, the star-spangled banner waves over the scene. Thus his children are trained to consider, that home is not only the most patriotic, but for them the happiest, place in the country. Enviable fathers! would that thousands of others would go and do likewise!

III. — IRRITABILITY OF TEMPER.

THERE is perhaps as much fault in the management of a child's temper as in any one thing relating to domestic discipline. When the temper of a quite young child is once roused, he is a perfect rebel. Nothing but absolute strength can restrain his squirming body. He cannot be reasoned with at this age, and especially in this condition. What can be done? Nothing but to wait till the little tempest has gone down, as we wait for that of the weather to get exhausted. Let no perturbed feelings appear in the actions or faces of bystanders, if it can possibly be helped. Especially let the person in immediate care strive for patience in the heart, and serenity on the countenance. Let there be soft, sweet soothings, — no loud exclamations. Sometimes the attention may be diverted to some attractive object, and the trouble pass away. But be sure that there shall be no responsive excitement of any kind in others around. Every child is born with the resentful emotion slumbering in his nature. With all care, it will sometimes start forth. But love and a wise self-possession will be adequate to the emergency.

Above all others, parents should not put to this element the kindling spark of their own irascible dispositions. Yet how often is this the case! The child, for instance, is at his interesting work, — mischief so called; and he breaks a choice vase, or soils some fancy-work. Now, the parent is any thing but the self-possessed and patient one that provokes not children to wrath. To be startled at the accident is pardonable; but what a look! what a tone! Ah! what a hand on that unintentional misdoer! Then the child, catching the baleful spirit, — with what look and tone and action he images back the angry parent! How is the tender, the sweet, and the lovely scorched and withered away by such outbursts of the nether elements!

"But I can't help this temper" is the excuse. "I inherited it from my own parents: they didn't manage it well in my own childhood. Indeed I wish I could govern it as I should." Can you not do it, my friend? Let us see. Suppose you have company, much-respected friends, and a vase is broken or some fancy-work soiled; then how soft the admonition! The very scolding is as sweet as music; and the visitors go away with the idea and exclamation, "What an amiable disposition!"

Your excuse is, that you cannot maintain calmness under a sudden excitement of feeling. As to this, let us have another illustration: A careless father leaves his naked razor on the table, on some brief absence from the room. The little child is entertaining himself with his own resources. The mother, that mother who was yesterday so hasty spirited, is occupied with her affairs. At length, her eye catches a glimpse of the little experimenter; and, behold! he, curious creature, wishing to know something about razors, has the glittering implement in his hand. His tender finger is within a hair's breadth of the fearful edge. Well, she is suddenly surprised, far more than yesterday: she is dreadfully alarmed. But does she start and spring, and startle the unconscious innocent? Does she scream out and catch hold? Oh, no! At the least joggle of that tiny, unsteady hand, the finger may slip, and there will be a bloody gash; or the implement may drop on his tender foot, and he will be maimed for life. What now? "Hold it fast, darling; let mother have it; hold it fast." What astonishing self-possession! How engaging her smile! how winning her tones! and her tread is as soft as a rose-leaf lighting on the verdure beneath; and the child, charmed and drawn by such sweet, motherly magnetism, renders up the deadly thing, and is safe. Now, why cannot this parent realize, that the pricking temper, the deeply cutting anger, indulged over and over again by the child, makes wounds in the tender spiritual framework, which, hidden from the world's eye, may last on and last on, and be very sore, long after gashes from inanimate steel shall have been healed? Woe to that mother or father, woe to that elder sister or brother, whose own uncontrolled temper shall intensify or occasion such anguish in the young and helpless soul!

IV. — CHILDREN AT TABLE.

THERE is one time and one place at which an indulged and mismanaged family generally exhibit about their worst. It is the meal-time and the table. How often are they the occasion at which the lower nature in the child, the animal, manifests its claws, its teeth, and its quarrelsome voracity! The call is given for the morning, mid-day, or evening repast, — no matter which; and now how the creatures rush to their feeding! What a scraping and squeaking of chairs, as they drag them up or pull them back! What rattle and racket, as they creep up or tumble on! Then what hastening to the onset! — cries for this or that! or, without a cry, they dash into one thing, or slash across another. Then there is the hue perhaps, especially at the daintier articles, "Mother, he's getting it almost all : I sha'n't have any." The reply is snapped back: "I say I'm not getting it all; but you got it almost all yesterday, and I'm going to have my share to-day." Indeed, all law and order, if there ever were any, are entirely upset; and perhaps some dishes are upset too.

There is no more strength of authority in that distracted and custom-hardened mother than there is in a wreath of steam curling up from the hot cookery. It is possible that the father's grum voice and stern look may command order; or, very likely, they may not. He perhaps considers the meals, and the management thereat, the mother's affair, unless the uproar becomes quite insupportable.

Then he simply exclaims, " Pshaw, pshaw! what a noise you make!" And he meekly puts down his food with Yankee, tavern-like velocity, and scuds out of his own home, away from his own empire, as if to save his ears.

As it regards these unmannerly and unmanageable children at the table, there is one simple rule. It is this: If a child does not come quietly, and take his own proper place, and there wait till he is helped; and then, if he should not be satisfied with what he is helped to in ordinary circumstances,— indeed, should he behave in any way such as would put you to the blush (with company), — *send him away instantly.* Do not threaten, as the majority of parents do, " You shall leave the table, if you don't behave better. I tell you, you *shall.*" What cares he? He knows it is nothing but breath : he has heard the threat ever since he can remember. No : let the rule be understood and established ; let it be acted on as instantaneously as the report follows the flash of a gun, — only with perfect gentleness, as well as decision, on your part. There should be no harshness of voice, or roughness of hand : indeed there will be no need of it, if such shall be the well-understood rule.

It may be said, that the child, by some inadvertence, may make an unintentional mistake. Very well : then the certain penalty will prevent future carelessness. This would avert, perhaps, a similar carelessness and ill manners, and confusion of countenance, when there shall be company. Indeed, so train your child, and it may certainly be done, that you shall just motion with your finger for him to leave the table, and he shall instantly obey and be gone ; and all so quietly, that the persons present, possibly, shall be first made aware, by his vacant place, that he has left. Thus, under all circumstances at the table, you are at ease; you have no fear; and your children are being formed at once to easy and appropriate manners, whatever be the company.

Do not, however, follow the example of a brother-clergyman. "I have complied with your rule already," he remarked, as I was commending this method of discipline. "I have sent my children away for bad behavior. But I find they like nothing better; for they have then a capital time in the kitchen with the maids." — "Did you send them into the kitchen?" I asked in reply. — "Oh, yes! where else should they go?" — "Not there," I rejoined; "for, while you and the mother are eating the pudding, they will there be eating the pie or the cake, or whatever nice bit the good-humored girls can hunt up to tickle their palates, and gain their favor. Oh, no! that is not the way. Put each in a corner by himself, with no fellowship from anybody, or any thing but his own memory and heart and conscience. Let him feel how very lonely and how very cold it is to be shut away from the genial table, and the warm, loving hearts around; and such discipline will not often need to be repeated."

Why should there not be perfect propriety of manners at home, and in all its unguarded privacy, as well as anywhere else? There should certainly be respectful manners and language to parents there, and particularly at the table. There should be courtesy also to brothers and sisters; and here is a very special opportunity, which ought not to be neglected. Indeed, the table is about the best possible schooling-place for manners. Every day, regularly, it presents opportunity for theory and practice. The table is the place where the sweetest family affections may be cultivated, and the heart flow around from one to another, as nowhere else. Every meal should present something new of intelligence brought by those who come from abroad. With a little effort, with a little regard for the great ends of existence, certainly this might be realized to an extent far beyond what has ever been before in the majority of families. Let the meal be the simplest: should necessity compel, it may be nothing but bread and fruits; and yet there may be as rich a pastime to the intellect and heart as the most abundant wealth, or even royal revenues, could afford.

The table is the special place and scene of what is called " hospitality." This word generally has reference to those who come in from without; but it may have a higher meaning, and be applied to those who abide together within. Each family, and loving and beloved soul in it, may have at the table, and at every meal, another and new occasion for fresh hospitality to the dear souls around. This consists in *utterance*, with the common desire to entertain, or in *listening*, with a desire to be entertained; for it is hospitable, as well as *courteous*, to listen, — inasmuch as, when one thinks he can do good by speech, he likes to be heard. How beautiful might these table-manners be, in all they comprehend as to the mental as well as the material man!

Thus a family would be prepared for propriety, grace, kind feeling, anywhere. They might sit down in the humblest abode, or with the rudest people, and still put them at perfect ease; and this without at all participating in their rudeness. They might sit in the highest circles of our country, indeed with nobles and princes, and make themselves agreeable and respected by their charming gracefulness, joined with their pure Christian simplicity.

Finally: do not forget the rule, SEND THEM INSTANTLY AWAY.

SUGGESTIONS

ON

THE DISCIPLINE OF THE OBSERVING FACULTIES.

NOTE.

To leave moral training for the present, attention is asked to a subject not so absolutely important as the preceding, but one in which parents should have a lively interest. Many years ago, the present writer, in lecturing on early intellectual culture, earnestly urged the discipline of the observing faculties. He then had not the remotest idea, that this discipline, as an indispensable requisite, would be so long neglected; for it was at that time practised in European schools, and advocated also by eminent writers in our own country. More than twenty years, however, have elapsed since his first humble efforts and sanguine expectations; and yet but little progress comparatively has been made in this direction. In preparing this volume, it came forcibly to mind, that a much-needed help might be rendered to the family, and indirectly to the school, by some practical suggestions on this part of education. By the aid of a single written passage and some brief notes, some former utterances, which were mostly extemporaneous, have been introduced into this work, interspersed with fresh matter suggested by more recent circumstances.

It may be further premised, to prevent any possible misconception, that it is not intended to crowd upon childhood what is above its ability. Some of the proposed exercises are perhaps more appropriate to youth. Most of them, however, might be entered into by children of various ages, in company with the parents themselves, all in mutual cultivation of the observing faculties. These suggestions are presented by one who has read and thought much on these subjects, and who has no interest but the best good of the community, older and younger. Will parents, will all readers, consider them with candor, and ask themselves, without any sort of prejudice, whether they are not sustained by reason and plain common sense? Most especially are they entreated to observe their bearing on success in business and most of the practical affairs in life.

SUGGESTIONS

ON

THE DISCIPLINE OF THE OBSERVING FACULTIES.

THE BEGINNING.

THE intellectual development of the human being begins as soon as he can open his eyes, and put forth his little hand, — as soon as his senses come in contact with the material world. From this time onward, he is continually gaining knowledge, and being prepared for his future of life, usefulness, and enjoyment. It is said, that all the simple elements of knowledge and the best part of man's education are obtained by the time he is five years of age. These foundations are mainly laid at home. The work is, or should be, under the supervision of the parents. This education, however, goes on, whether they attend to it or not. Indeed, the child will be continually educating himself. It may be truly said, that the first and the most important part of man's intellectual culture, as things have been, is self-culture. Now, this fostering from kindly nature, this forth-putting and forth-grasping of the infant faculties, may be exceedingly assisted by the parents and other older members of the family, if they did but think of it, and would but give themselves to it. Help, in this primary home institution, is as valuable as it is in the public seminaries to which the mind is afterward introduced. In the majority of homes, however, this assistance is casually and poorly rendered. It is because parents have the notion that they have nothing to do with intellectual development. This they suppose belongs only to the schools. If a child asks a question about any thing new to his curiosity, he may be kindly answered. If he persistently puts many questions, he is patiently borne with, or perhaps hastily hushed or snapped off. The parents have not the least suspicion, that, in replying to such questions, they are really exercising tutorships and professorships as important, to say the least, as any in college. Indeed, it may be affirmed with absolute truth, that as schools have generally been conducted, especially for little children, the education mostly stops at the school threshold; at least, it begins to be exceedingly hindered, as will plainly appear.

KNOWLEDGE WITHOUT BOOKS.

Just watch a babe, and see what Nature, or rather his own divinely devised constitution, prompts him to do; and let us gather useful hints from the observation. As soon as there is any visual discernment, there is a separation of one thing from another, and the reception of distinct ideas. The little one leaves the maternal lap, for what? — to work, and to get knowledge to prepare him for more and more work. He creeps about the room, not only for the pleasure of muscular action, but to seek for new objects to his curiosity; hunting for prey, if we may so speak, as food to his awakened and craving perceptions. Every thing he gets hold of is a subject of interest, — a fund of entertainment; and, though his mother perhaps thinks not of it, it is a source of most valuable instruction. We cannot just yet say of him, that "he who runs may read;" but we may say, that he who creeps can, — can read the great book of perceptible and practical knowledge open boundlessly before him, just as fast and far as he can get at it. Toeing and kneeing it along, he lays hold of every thing within the touch and the crook of his fingers. Why? he wants knowledge, and he will have it. First, the thing, — the individual: it is separate from some other thing he perceives, and he wants to know about it as another and distinct object. Then the several perceptive powers come into action; finding out the various qualities, — figure, color, size, weight, — as they are peculiar to each individual thing. Thus the child ranges through the room; and, when in due time he mounts to the top of his feet, he runs about the house, and soon out-doors, and then round about the premises, all the time after knowledge, — knowledge of objects, qualities, operations, uses. Before the little looker and hunter is four years old, he is acquainted with hundreds of things, — perhaps, we might say, thousands. He knows nothing about the book, it may be; but is he deficient in language? By no means: objects are distinguished by names; qualities, by appropriate terms. What riches of language are his, even now, though he may never have been at school, and cannot read a word! All this time, he has been in training for the duties and enjoyments of maturer life. He has been studying the Creator's perfect works, and unconsciously finding the steps which lead up to the Most

Wise and Most Loving. He has been acquainting himself with the things also made by human hands, and examining the materials of which they are composed. This is in preparation for the time when he himself shall make similar things, and will need accurate knowledge of fabrics and materials as to qualities and fitness for specific purposes.

INDUSTRIAL EFFORTS.

Nay, farther, our little beginner at life is something more than a learner: he is a maker. He is at his mechanics too. See him putting this with that in rude efforts at construction! Give him a dozen blocks, and he is in absolute blessedness at work; building up and pulling down, and altering, his wall or house, or whatever else he may be striving to imitate. How wonderfully industrious, imitative, and constructive! He wants to do every thing he sees others do. Give him little tools, fitted to his little fingers, and how delighted! How he skips off, all glee, to his miniature business! All these applications of his strength, and trials of his skill, are instincts and impulses to prepare him for the labors, duties, and pleasures of life. And the parents ought all the time to sympathize with him; lending a hand, now and then, to help just enough and no more; catching hints from instructive Nature, and carrying out her plans far beyond what the child's unassisted mind could think of in his own behalf. But they do no such thing. On the contrary, they cut off the little learner from the very education he was getting, as well as he could, almost all alone. They practically declare, "Nature, you do not know as much as old usage does, — usage begun in ignorance, and continued in stupidity."

AN ABUSE OF NATURE.

But let us more particularly consider what is done. Oh the sad change which comes over this childhood's dream, or rather over this contented, sweet reality! This is what we do, — we, grown-up and pretendedly grown-wiser people: we catch up the active, looking, learning, working, and manufacturing, happy little creature, and clap him, together with twenties, thirties, forties, or fifties besides, into a wooden box, hardly, in some instances, large enough to hold them without jamming and hurting one against the other; and fasten him upon a seat, out of the reach of the many objects he has been in the midst of, and which he has been doing with, as Nature intended. Yes, there we fasten him, or permit our agent, the school-committee or the school-teacher, to do it; and we make him bend his neck, and fix his eyes on a plain, dry surface of paper. This he must not cut, fold, crumple, or variously shape, in the way of cultivating his manufacturing abilities. No: he must look straight down upon this metamorphosis of cotton. Were it but the rags out of which it came, many-shaped, many-hued, there would be something to hold the eye; but what does he see now? Words, words, words; little, black, immovable images, which he cannot get his fingers under. What cares he for them? Nature made him to care for things, and for words too, just so far as they stand for the things he has to do with, or can have any clear idea of. He, indeed, has an appetite, if we may so speak, for words, so far as they convey any ideas; but we do not consult this appetite, but give him the words all tasteless of meaning. When I say this, I do not mean to convey, that no explanations at all are ever given, but that none scarcely are given, in a large majority of schools, take the country through, in immediate connection with the things to which they belong. Before the child enters school, it is always things; then, words. At school, it is first words, and then things; that is, if the pupil shall happen to come across them. Otherwise, he must go without such substantial acquaintance. Now, this ought not so to be. This period, lent by Nature to prepare for future industry and livelihood, ought not to be so unprofitably and wretchedly spent. In all common sense and true philosophy, this paper-deadening, ink-blinding delusion should be put away. But what shall take its place? Realities, life, thought, action, intelligence; just what the child has been forced to leave at his own home. This might be done, and how easily and cheaply done besides! Really it would not cost, on the whole, so much as school-weariness or school-hate costs, when it breaks over bounds, and runs wild into mischief.

PROFITABLE SCHOOLING.

Let our primary schoolrooms, and indeed the higher schoolrooms, be well provided with shelves and boxes. Let these be filled with all sorts of productions of nature and art; specimens of all sorts of wood and metals; all kinds of cloth and leather, or any other fabric,— indeed, of every thing which can well be brought into a school, and put in some proper receptacle. Let each one of these objects be a subject for examination by classes, in convenient order, under the direction of the teacher. In this way, the plan begun by Nature at home would be carried out, and carried out much farther than could possibly be at home under ordinary circumstances; as many objects would be supplied by the scholars from different families, which could not be had, excepting as each was found in a different home. All the perceptive faculties would here find delightful occupation, and be continually gaining in strength. Children would hardly be tired of such observation, due regard being given to their comfort and constitutional power of attention. Indeed, if rightly managed, they would enter heartily into minute examinations, and comparisons of one thing with another; for there might be a healthful and spirited emulation in the exercise. It may be farther remarked, that the words designating the object in hand, and its qualities and uses, must come into the occasion. These the children learn just as readily as they learn at home the name of the lamp, and that it is bright and hot; or the terms belonging to any thing else. Language is not lost, but rather most richly gained,

by this use of the time. Furthermore, just
consider the practical utility of this mode of
education. What a wide and minute acquaintance is formed with things, as necessaries, comforts, and luxuries, in living, or as appertaining
to the various affairs of business! How the
quality of the material and of the manufacture
of a commodity will be compared with the quality of another of the same kind; so that, by the
time the child shall be old enough to leave
school, he shall have run through the whole
range of objects ever used in ordinary life, and
be able to detect the minutest differences between one and another of the same sort! With
such a training, it would be utterly impossible
for manufacturer or trader to impose an inferior
production on the purchaser. He must proportion his price to the quality, or keep his goods
on his hands. With the ignorance of commodities in which people have been kept until grown
up, and obliged to purchase for themselves, how
continually have they been subjected to impo-
sitions on their credulity, and to consequent
annoyance of spirit! It has really taken a lifetime to obtain that practical knowledge of qualities and fitnesses which might be acquired
by boys and girls before they should be half

through their teens, were the common-sense and time-saving method above explained adopted. How also are the poor now imposed upon! They must take a second or third rate article at a very little reduction from the price of the best, to make a small saving. Yet, in the longrun, theirs are the dearest purchases of all. But, with such an education, there could scarcely be any imposition on anybody. The children of the poor, in our common schools, are equally learners with those of the rich. If those who are pinched for money must seek the cheapest thing, they will know exactly its comparative value, and will either have fair terms, or go to some competitor more favorable to their circumstances. Then the struggle would be among the manufacturers to see who should excel, — who should go ahead in improvement, — as knowing that the purchasers have been trained from very infancy to detect imperfections. Then the trader could not deceive the buyer, if the manufacturer should succeed in deceiving him. Indeed, retailer, jobber, wholesale dealer, and manufacturer must all be honest men, selling at prices exactly just; that is, according to quality, all other circumstances being equitably considered. If every article in a dry-goods store or a grocery, or any other furnishing establishment, were thus put to the test of minute examination and comparison, the reign of that old hollow-hearted despot whose power is in his own pretence and in the ignorance of his subjects — the reign of King Sham — would be ended.

LOSS AND GAIN.

Thus much might easily be done in our schools; yes, and save enough money by the "operation," as trading people have the term, to pay the whole school-tax. Just think of it, friends! — how much the majority of people actually lose out of pocket by overpaying for poor commodities! Or, if price and quality do go honestly together, how much uncomfortableness is often occasioned to the body, and trouble to the spirit, by these cheap imperfections! How often, too, the purse suffers, in the long-run, by all the rips, breakages, and good-for-nothingness for which the few dollars or few cents saved are far from making up! Who has not had occasion to feel the truth of the saying, "The cheapest things are the dearest"? Just look round your premises, and take a distinct observation of all the various necessaries, comforts, luxuries, and elegances there gathered. Consider the ceaseless rush of wearables, eatables, drinkables, and burnables into your household receptacles. Then reflect that all this mixed and continuous avalanche of earthly matter is sweeping through your doors from the beginning to the end of married life, half a century perhaps and more, costing to moderate fortunes, for fifty years, fifty thousand dollars at least, and to others twice or four times that amount; and then reflect how often through this long period the twain and their dependents have been mistaken, have been cheated, or somehow have lost in their bargainings, in consequence of not having their senses about them; at least one sense wide open and sharp, — that is, the sight. Yes, friends, take all these absolute realities into a clear comprehension, and then tell me whether the shelves and boxes of specimen goods at the schoolroom, and the careful inspection and comparison of them by the pupils, in the course of all the long years passed there, are nothing but a theorist's *whim*.

But, alas! even if you should think this commodity project not a whim, but rather an all-important requisite, it would be quite in vain as schools are now arranged. Even if parents, committees, and teachers should all be convinced of the value of the proposition, it might take no short time to get it into action. Who does not know that public improvements, however well acknowledged, are often postponed for years? Inconvenient and unhealthy schoolrooms in cities, and miserable old schoolhouses in the country, prove this fact. However, the better time is coming, as a few schools here and there in our country bear witness. In the mean time, good parents, what shall prevent you from going into this commodity training at once in your own families? Indeed your children are at it now, all by themselves, — even the youngest creeper on the carpet. They only want a little assistance. Their senses are all alive and awake; their observing faculties are at their appointed work. The difficulty is, there are so many new things all about in this freshly entered world, that they do not work long enough on one piece of matter; they are not thorough. Now, what these little candidates for purchases and house-keeping want is your help and companionship at inspection. How much can be learned of real substantial knowledge, even before the child shall arrive at the school-going age! Without any help at all, except his own keen senses or the eager perceptives behind them, he becomes marvellously knowing at four or five years of age. Now, amid all your gettings of new things, what a constant opportunity is there for him to get an understanding of them, if you will but stop to show him! What ample time is there during the three meals a day, at the table, for the inspection of things in use thereupon, and for talk about things which have been seen otherwhere! Indeed, friends, you may take your children along through your whole house-world, and over and over again, searching every thing as thoroughly as air, light, and heat search them, by the time they shall come to the edge of their youthful years. Even a seven-year-old errand-doer would have something like a mature judgment as to the poor, the better, and the best, at the store where he carries your cents, dimes, and quarters, to bring you back, as you hope, the best thing to be had for the money. You would find, I can affirm without fear of contradiction, the immortal adage to be true, even of a child, that "knowledge is power,"— power over a store-keeper or any other money-maker. Just try the plan at once, my friends, and be convinced. You will then have something to talk about with your children, not so much to grumble about, and not so much time for grumbling. Finally, when you shall have thoroughly proved the value and the pleasure of this thing, — learning in the home seminary, — then try all your influence for a change in the school. Both institutions earnestly working together, be assured that all sorts of producers would have to go ahead toward pefection, and trade would be compelled to be honest. Adulteration, that vile deceiver, that sometimes awful poisoner, would be cornered, starved out, and have to give up. Old and mighty Sham, as was intimated before, would have to abdicate, and his line would perish.

Much more is yet to be said about the investigation of material things. It has happened to be convenient to present the subject just now in one respect, — that of quality and comparative fitness for uses, — a sort of profit-and-loss view of the matter. I shall now take up this object-study somewhat methodically, and in various relations. All, however, will have a bearing, more or less, on practical utility.

INFANTILE ACTIVITY.

The exercise of the observing faculties — object-study — begins in early infancy, prompted by the inborn instincts. Some hints appertaining to this tenderest age may be of benefit: so they are here given intermediately as we pass along.

Set it down, friends, as a fact, that your children want things substantial, and palpable to the senses, from the time they are put on the floor, from the mother's lap. They must have them at first, or nothing. Let them, therefore, have what they want; but it must be judiciously and properly. The infant is pleased with that which he can grasp, and shake about, and put to his mouth. But do not, like some ignorant parents, give him what may be hurtful, — a painted toy, for instance; so that he shall be in danger of sucking the paint, and of being poisoned: for the taste is one of the first avenues to infantile knowledge and enjoyment, and there is a sucking instinct. Put into his hands little hard things of different shapes, and made of ivory, or some other clean, firm substance, which may be found perhaps at the toy-shop; or things of solid wood, which you can carve out yourself. When he shall fairly get upon the floor, there to be seated like a monarch on his throne, or to move about like a mechanic in his shop, provide him with little blocks, and other manageable things, to pile up and toss about. When he shall be old enough to try any thing like building with them, some one should show him how, and help his beginning. Few probably need this hint; yet there are some too busy with work or amusements, or too indolent, to stoop a few moments to the incipient constructor, if he is not in the way of their feet, or makes no disturbing cries. Any thing which will not harm him, and which he himself cannot injure, might be within his domain or his workshop. Pray, have the good sense not to let him have, even to gain a moment's quiet, what he may tear or deface, such as the yet-unread newspaper or a valuable book. He must understand that he can never have such things, at least unless there are those of the kind devoted to his special use alone. You will save a great deal of time and trouble by firmness in this matter. In process of the months, he becomes a traveller on all-fours about the room: he is in search of curiosities and adventures. It is now far better to keep entirely out of his reach things he must not touch, than to be ever anxiously on the watch, and perpetually stopping, thwarting, and irritating the headlong discoverer. As for the rest which cannot be put aside, such as the stove or the fireplace, and the implements belonging to them, just let him understand, that it is your will, *which cannot be changed*, that he must never touch them. If necessary, just let him get, under your careful watch, an uncomfortably hot, but not a burnt finger a few times; and he will perceive why he must not go too far in that direction.

SYMPATHY WANTED.

Enough has been said perhaps to indicate how a child may be entertained and instructed for the first year. As the second comes on, he begins to run about, and to go anywhere, and get at every thing; and you are put to your activity to keep him within safe bounds. He is perpetually finding new things. His brain is too weak to be kept very long at one single object: so it is a happy provision, that curiosity should carry him quickly from one thing to another. Nevertheless, let him hold on to what he has, as long as he will; the longer, the better: for thus he will form the habit of concentrated attention, preparing him to stick to a lesson till he thoroughly learns it, or to any other pursuit in the future till he shall have accomplished it. By and by, when he shall discover some new and curious thing, he will run with it to you if he can, or bring you to it, to show you what a wonderful discovery he has made. He is a social being, such as he is to be, or ought to be, in all his after-life. It is worthy of remark, and of gratitude also to the good Creator, how children want the presence, the attention, and especially the sympathy, of others. Above all things, in gratifying curiosity, and getting knowledge, and doing their little play-work, they crave sympathy. How this infantile innocence instructs far-off manhood and womanhood, and rebukes solitary and cold self-seeking! Your child wants sympathy: give it to him on the spot. He will be satisfied with a very little. Do not turn him abruptly off, unless the house should be on fire, or somebody is in agonizing pain, and must have you at once. Look, as he holds up his new-found treasure: look! perhaps you will learn something yourself: for children often find out interesting items of knowledge which their parents had been utterly ignorant of before. Then dismiss the novelty-finder with a tender word and a kind look, and he will run away as happy as ever Agassiz was after having discovered and lectured about some new species of fish; for genial science delights to impart as well as to find.

INDIVIDUALIZING.

But your child has begun to talk: he calls things by name; that is, if, in all patience, you will tell him what the names are. Now or soon, you may help him to cultivate into strength and acuteness the most important perceptive faculty of his mind: it is the individualizing faculty. The phrenologists name it "individuality." All qualities of material things which fit them for special uses inhere in separate individual objects. Certain qualities are bunched together, and thus form a certain species of things. Now, unless the sense distinctly detects and gets hold of the thing, the qualities and uses cannot be apprehended. So, one of the very first observing powers put in action is that of individuality. It is not some new quality, but some new and distinct object, which the child drives at and lays hold of; and then he looks for its properties. Some have this faculty constitutionally much stronger than others. Many a boy and girl, many a man and woman, go along the roads in a country place, or the streets of a city, with their eyes half shut, or gazing about with a vacant stare, or fastened straightforward upon nothing. Others observe every thing, and gain knowledge at every step and at every turn of the eye. Such being the constitutional differences in children, it will be well for parents to attend early to this matter. Perhaps they themselves are deficient in this individualizing ability, and it is time that they should make up the deficiency.

THE OBJECT-GAME.

As a mutual benefit, and pleasure indeed, let parent and child have a sort of game at finding objects. It may be called " the thing-game," or, if you please, " the object-game." The wall, ceiling, window, floor, carpet, table, chairs, and so on, will probably first strike attention, and be named. Soon, all the prominent objects of the room will be exhausted. Then there will be a scramble for something more. Objects will be discovered which otherwise would not have met the eye, or have been thought of. The head of a nail, a shred of cloth, the minutest thread, or any particle of matter: a spot or mark on the furniture or wall, or any thing else: any thing which may bear a name, — will be detected one after another: and he is the victor who shall find the minutest and most out-of-the-way thing to which may be put a name, and the last thing to be found. At another time, the same game may be played with objects in the yard, or anywhere around the house, or as far away as the sight can reach from door or window. Different apartments in the house may be made the scene of the game. If the time be the dark evening or a winter's cold day, let the trial be, who shall call to recollection the most objects in some other room in the house, or in the more distant shed or barn. What an inventory will thus be made of the implements and various goods of the household! You might go farther, and call to recollection what may have been noticed in a neighbor's domicile, or anywhere else. Thus, in mere exciting pastime, you will develop in your child and in yourselves the central and most important faculty of the intellect. You will all be trained to keep your eyes open, to look, to see, and to separate one thing from another; and thus to obtain knowledge of new and distinct things wherever you go. How keen at catching objects at a glance will you become, if you only try! You know how the sailor will discover a ship at the distant horizon when it seems but a speck, but which the undisciplined passenger could not possibly perceive. It is because he has been for years searching the ocean's surface for any object which may break the blank uniformity, and especially for his eye's love, — a sail. His success at such perception is a matter of discipline and use. Just so the sight of children might be trained to acuteness of observation among the objects on the land, if parents would set themselves and their children about it. Of course, as was intimated before, there will be differences in accomplishment according to differences in organic constitution.

QUALITIES: FORM.

Next, after individualizing the world of matter around, comes the learning of the forms of things. These forms can be seen by the eye in the light, — can be felt by the hand in the dark: they are the subjects of two senses. Soon will the child learn the ideas and the names, — long and short, square and round. Indeed, you may cheaply provide blocks exhibiting all the various geometrical figures; and the child in due time (for I would force nothing) might learn the various geometrical names. At his impressible age, it will be as easy for him to fasten on his memory a scientific term as any other word, if there is only a real visible object under it. How easily, then, will he learn whether any object his sense falls on is most like a square, triangle, cube, parallelogram, sphere, cone, pyramid, or any thing else! I need not here run through the several geometrical figures and names. You may easily get a book, and look at them; and the advantage to yourselves and children will amply repay the trouble.

SIZE AND MEASUREMENT.

To proceed with qualities: next comes the size of things. The child soon perceives this, without your telling him that one object is larger or smaller than another. All he wants from you are words to designate differences in dimension. Yes: he does want, or rather need, something else. He needs training to accuracy in discriminating the size and bulk of different things. Let him then have, when he shall be old enough, a two-foot rule such as carpenters use, or the household yard-stick, marked off into feet and inches; and set him to measuring objects, — whatever or wherever he pleases, bating all harm. He can find the length and breadth of the floor; the length, width, and height of furniture. Indeed, have him measure the dimensions of any thing he may put his rule against, within or around the house. When he shall be old enough, furnish him with a ten-foot pole, or a rope, or an iron chain of longer stretch; and, with this, set him to finding the length and breadth of a field, or the distance between your own house and the next neighbor's, or the school-house or the church. Thus your boy is becoming a surveyor before he knows it. This procedure will not be a dry task to him, unless you make it so: it will seem to make a man of him, and he cannot but like it. I see no impropriety, moreover, in a sister's taking a part in such outdoor, healthy, and instructive action. Certainly, all in-door exercises in such measurements will fall within the proprieties of female life, and much in the uses of it. Why not make a sort of competition and game of this quality of size? Let a guess be made as to the length, breadth, or height of any thing; and then see who comes nearest to the fact by the measure. Your boys and girls will like it; and so will you, if you have any of your young sportiveness still left in your soul.

But some will inquire, What practical advantage can this possibly be in the future? It is replied, that the active business of almost every one depends more or less on off-hand and immediate decisions, based on a knowledge of things. The farmer does not often scientifically survey the portion of a field he intends to plough up for a crop. He decides on the quantity through his previous knowledge of comparative proportions. The more accurately he can judge of lengths and breadths, the nearer will be his work to his wishes. Oftentimes, this kind of judgment will come into play in respect to spaces and distances. Again, in buying and selling loads and piles of commodities, men often guess at the dimensions, or judge by the eye, without definite numerical measurement. He, therefore, who shall have the truest perception of size will have the advantage. In the affairs of a household, moreover, such as the cutting and repairing of garments and the proportioning of quantities in cookery, the faculty of size comes into most useful requisition. Why, therefore, shall it not be assiduously developed from early life onward, to the saving of work, time, money, and comfort, quite worth the while, take the life through?

WEIGHT.

Now comes the quality of weight. In a most incidental, unlesson-like. and playful way, you can teach your child, boy or girl, the difference between one thing and another as to weight. Let him lift first one object, and then another; so that he may perceive the difference in the pressure upon his hands. You can tell him, that this pressure is weight, and that one thing weighs more than another. He will learn, too, that the difference, in different kinds of things, does not depend on size. In due time, you can show him what it does depend on. Provide some scales. These will not cost more than a few cigars, or any other luxury which you exhaust in the using, or some little piece of finery quickly worn out; but the scales will last for years, and outweigh their own price a thousand times over in this educational usefulness. With these let him weigh all the various commodities proper to be put into them. Do not make a task of the matter, but rather a pastime, which you may join in yourselves. In the first place, have each one present take the commodity in hand, and lift it up and down, and guess how much it weighs, or rather try to form an accurate judgment about it. Then put it into the scale, and see who comes nearest to the fact. Thus the little company, parents and children, have not only entertainment, but gain knowledge; and a special faculty is disciplined for future and valuable use in the affairs of life. It would be easy to show the special application of this training to practical purposes, as in the case of the other faculties and qualities. Thinking readers can readily illustrate for themselves.

COLOR.

There is a special faculty likewise to observe color. Such different properties of objects as form and weight must certainly require the use of a specific power: so also must color; for this differs from every other property in nature. This faculty of color may be disciplined to marvellous acuteness and enjoyment, if pains are only taken with it. Of all the appearances of matter, the child earliest observes and delights in color. It is the color of the fire and the lamp which so early attracts the infant eye: so of other objects one after another. Bright and dazzling colors are his joy. As his age shall warrant, teach him the names of the various distinct colors. By the help of a book, if you need one, you may be somewhat methodical in your instructions. You can give him the names of the three primary colors, then of the secondary colors; and, at length, of all the various colors made up from these; together with the many hues, tints, and tinges which have names. Provide patterns of cloth as copies; and, from these, let the child get the idea and name of the distinctive colors. This will be a pleasant matter, if you choose to make it so. You may get up a color-game, as you do with the other qualities. Take any object of an indeterminate color, and see who will quickest find the standard color which it most nearly resembles. See who shall name the colors, hues, or tinges, to the greatest number of objects according to some text-book. Here are the things both of art and of nature, innumerable, all around, with colors of all sorts: what a source of entertainment and discipline for the special faculty, if parents will but think of it, and go at the work, or rather the sport! The training of this faculty is of singular importance to those who have much to do with dry goods, and especially to ladies who are the principal purchasers. I once knew a farmer's wife, the mother of an infant boy, and of a little girl perhaps three years old, at the time I have in mind. She had no help but that of her own hands, and of this little bud of a maid. Among other things, she must make, mend, and alter garments. She could not well run up stairs to a closet or drawer for a piece of cloth, whenever she might want it: so she had all the various fabrics of wool, cotton, or silk, done up respectively in separate parcels by themselves. Not only so, but, if I recollect aright, there was a subdivision of fabrics, according to color. So, when in her work the mother needed a particular cloth of a particular color, she sent the little active and willing girl away up stairs for it. If she made a mistake in the selection, she had to go back and forth till she got the right little roll. The result was, that the child became exceedingly discriminating in whatever belonged to cloths and their colors. She, at length, manifested remarkable taste as to the fitnesses and proprieties of dress. Her natural organization might have been favorable to such ability. Nevertheless, such an early use of the special faculty must have enhanced this prominent characteristic.

NATURE.

In this training to the observance and enjoyment of color, you will, of course, not omit the infinite variety in the aspects of nature. With sunshine and cloud, mountains, lowlands, woods, waters, and other features of nature, what a range for the eye! How it may be taught to fasten and feast on distinctive colors, and their many lights and shades!

FLOWERS.

The flowers cannot possibly be omitted; for these are among the first things which attract a child's admiring gaze. These will afford almost numberless lessons in discriminating colors. They may not be so practically useful as the lessons upon cloths; but the living and wonderful beauty will make them far more delightful. What a taste might be nurtured, what pleasure secured and continually enhanced, by a little pains! How easily might the delighted mind be carried, in due time, from the charm of the flowers into the rich botanical science which lies in their various characteristics, and in the leafy structure which they adorn!

Another special subject of notice is the various colors and hues of the different vegetable productions. What a difference between one kind of grain or grass and another! What changes of hue in the same kind, as the growth proceeds! Habituate your child to watch, day after day, as the invisible Painter varies the tints and tinges and shades. Direct his eye to all the appearances presented by the vegetable realm, as there may be cloud or sunshine, breeze or calm. Thus training him to observe Nature in all her many shows, you may fit him for landscape painting; at any rate, you will prepare him better to enjoy the painter's work. But, above all, you will educate him to delight in the matchless wonders of the all-perfect Hand.

GRAINS.

Furthermore: do not let the little learner go without knowing one grain from another, as to both stalk and kernel. It would be well to put each kind of grain into a little box or transparent vial, for convenient future observations. It is perfectly wonderful how much music or mathematics, and many other things, are learned, or rather are pretended to be learned, while the commonest and most useful things are left out of the catalogue of requirements. I once travelled in a stage-coach with a little girl, eleven years old, who was going from her dear home to a high-priced fashionable boarding-school, fifty miles away, to be educated. The schools close by her father's door—and they were quite good schools too — would not answer. I made some inquiries of the child as to the particulars of her course of instruction. Her studies seemed to me very remarkable; but she knew so little of them, that she could make no remark about them herself. We passed a large wheat-field, goldenly rich and beautiful; for it was just before the harvest. I inquired if she knew what grain that was; and she had no more idea of it than she would have had of the vegetation of the tropics, if she had been dropped suddenly down into the midst of it. She was equally ignorant of a great many other striking objects and useful things along the road. Just so, thousands of our young ladies go to school, spend money, tug at lessons, and learn words, and yet hardly know what their bread is made of. At least, they know not much about industrious Nature's primal and indispensable factory out in the fields.

TREES.

A word more about another kind of production. Your child learns, doubtless, very early, which is the apple or pear or peach or plum tree, — and how each looks, if such be near by; and can also tell the elms from the maples standing, it may be, at the door or along the street. But it is possible, unless you take some

little pains, — and certainly if you put him
into the school-prison early, and there keep
him, — that he will not advance much further
in his knowledge of trees. There is many a
boy who grows up without being able to name
the trees in a neighboring wood; and of qualities he is very much more ignorant still. As to
girls, the majority know next to nothing about
these magnificent monarchs of the vegetable
kingdom. They lift themselves all alive out of
the ground, and stretch out their leafy scep-
tres, and wear their foliaged crowns, and there
tower, — waiting to be looked at, admired, and
studied; and yet, with all their beauty and state-
liness, how unrecognized they remain! Now,
friends, parental readers, let it not be so with
your children, whether sons or daughters, if you
would have them truly educated. Turn their
attention to the difference, in form and general
appearance, between one species of tree and another. They will most readily learn the names.
Show them clearly the different parts of the
tree, and teach them the words designating
each part. According as the age permits, you
can have much conversation with them on the
philosophy of its growth and nature. I was
once walking on a farm with the owner's little

boy, five years of age; and he pointed out to my unnoticing sight, with a keen eye and the zest of a naturalist, a peculiar characteristic of a great oak near which we passed. That father, I found, made it a pastime to show his child the things of nature, and to make explanations about them; and I am very sure it was a pastime to my little companion and instructor.

But to proceed: take the little learner into the woods, and see what new trees you can find there, and help him to a knowledge of these. If you are ignorant yourself, become his fellow-learner.

LEAVES.

One thing, in particular, might be done to improve the observing powers in minuteness, and to prepare entertainment for the future. The leaf of one species of tree differs from that of another. Now, let the exact difference be noticed, and at length fixed in the memory. Let a number of leaves be culled from each tree, and thoroughly dried by pressure in a book; then when all the foliage has fallen under the cold, and the inclement winter has come, what fun, and instruction too, can you and your children have with the leaves! You can make it a pleasant game to see who shall best tell the name of the tree to which each kind of leaf belonged. It may take several games to associate some twenty or thirty of these little things, so variously shaped and notched, each with the name of its parent of the pasture or forest. Then, when the next vegetative season shall arrive, how sharp the young eyes will be after the different kinds of trees, each with its differently shaped foliage! The leaves of shrubs, plants, grains, and grasses might also be prepared in the same way for the winter's amusement and instruction. It would be a good plan, moreover, to provide little pieces of all sorts of wood; letting a portion of the bark remain as one of the distinctive marks. Thus the child and yourselves, companions as docile as he, will learn the difference between the color, fibre, and strength of one species of wood and those qualities in another species. He will come to know the kind of wood from its internal look, as well as from its external, with which he began. By this inspection, he will be gradually acquainting himself with all the various sorts of timber which in after-life he may have to do with, either as a manufacturer or a purchaser. As things have been, this valuable knowledge has been left to a life-long experience of mistakes and losses, mingled in with whatever successes may have come.

MINERALS.

Still further: you may lead your young looker into the mineral kingdom, and find many treasures there, before saying any thing about mineralogy. You may, however, give the term, if you please; and he will remember and like it at his age, as well as any other word. You may incidentally teach him mineralogical terms: only be sure to have them stand for visible and real objects. What makes children dislike these matters is the taking the life out of them, if they have any, by a hard lesson-task, without any intelligible explanation. In the first place, you can easily have at hand, for illustration, specimens of the several metals in common use; such as iron, lead, copper, silver, gold, and other metals; and also their various combinations. Let the differences, uses, and comparative values of these substances be shown, together with their original locations and conditions in the earth. How very much you might communicate, from time to time, about these minerals: storing treasures in the mind richer and more lasting than the precious metals themselves! Again: have your child hunt for rocks which are peculiar for size, shape, color, streaks, spots, or mossy pictures. Show him the different layers of earth, disclosed by a cut through a hill where a road passes, or in a river's bank. He has eyes, as well as a farmer, to notice how the productive soils differ from each other, and also from the barren strata beneath. Thus, from this early date onward, he will obtain that knowledge of land which is all-important to the agriculturist, and indeed is useful to any one who cultivates but a little patch of a garden. You may have a game together to see who shall find the greatest number of curious stones. Or, if you are at the water-side, try who shall be most successful in spying out beautiful pebbles. This slight beginning in mineralogical science may possibly lead to a zealous and thorough continuance. Many years ago, some crystals embedded in a lump of iron ore were pointed out to a youth. He was so surprised at their regularity and beauty, and with the fact that they had been hidden for ages in that entirely different and shapeless mass of matter, that his eyes were afterward put on the watch for similar things. This trivial circumstance first gave the start to one of the most distinguished mineralogists of our country, and the author of valuable treatises on the science. Now, if your boy shall not become eminent, he may, by your aid, become a minute observer of mineral substances. Ever afterward, his eye will be sharper to detect them, and his travelling be made interesting by bowlders in the pastures, stones by the wayside, or even gravel rattling beneath his carriage-wheels in the road.

It will be well to help your little fellow-rambler to begin a mineralogical cabinet, although this may seem too grand a phrase for the occasion. The rudest boards, and the lad's collection of curious pebbles or coarser stones to put upon them, will suffice to commence with, if there shall be nothing better. The very fact, that a particular depository has been prepared for such things, will induce effort to fill it up. Great pleasure, perhaps great usefulness, may grow in the future from this humble beginning. Should it be so, your son will thank you a thousand times for this first setting-out in the science which he got from a loving parent.

ANIMALS.

If the very ground beneath the feet can be made to yield so much to the early mind, how much more the living creatures which move above it! How delighted even infants are with the pictures of animals! What a marvel, then, are the substantial animate creatures themselves! These move about, and have a purpose in moving, as has the child himself. They *do* something, and there is a sort of wonder what they will do next. The household dog and cat are favorites, and the animals about the yard and barn are objects of interest, — all this before much instruction can be given. Nature is getting the pupil ready. In due season, and soon will this come to most, how much may be taught concerning the distinctive natures and habits of these tenants of the homestead! But the wider animal kingdom — curiosity cannot reach the end of this; but it can delightedly travel on and on, if instruction will only lead it forward a little. The birds, which make the spring so gladsome and the summer fields and groves so all alive, have specific forms, colors, notes, habits, histories. Now, the boys and girls might become knowing and acute in these various matters, just as well as to be so sharp-eyed after birds' nests, as most of them are. Indeed, young people in the country, if parents and teachers would only look to it, might make no small progress in ornithology before the customary school-years should be over. As for the larger four-footed creatures, there is not much chance at them, except through the happening of a menagerie or a wilderness. Some of the smaller quadrupeds, however, are within easy reach. The nimble, chirruping squirrel has several habits of his own. The opening curiosity would be just as ready to learn about these as to watch his freakish motions. Even rat and mouse might be made something of scientifically. Perhaps, if the truth were known of the skulks, they would seem very much less offensive. Even snakes and worms might also have a better repute with the associations. Let us save our children from a life-long disgust, if we can.

INSECT CURIOSITIES.

There is another division of the animal kingdom which spreads all around the home in every direction, — that of insects. How countless their species and varieties! There is no reason why the young should not be introduced into considerable acquaintance with the science of entomology, and this without hard and dry study. Even this long and strange scientific term would be no burden to the fresh memory, because it would mean something to it. What a trifle would a microscope cost for family use! so that, when any singular little creature should be found, there might be a minute and wondering inspection.

There is a country town, one of the roughest in New England, which was favored with a clergyman who well understood the true methods of education. Among other investigations, he devoted some of his leisure to entomology. Somehow, he inspired the people of the whole town. more or less, with his spirit, and especially the young. All eyes were opened and sharpened to discover some new bug or worm or butterfly; and happy was the little boy or girl who could run with some prize of the kind to the minister, receive his thanks, and get a peep through his microscope at the wonders. Now, if one man could exercise such an influence over a whole town six miles square, what might not be expected of young learners, were school-teachers in their separate districts, and parents at the homestead, all to get their perceptions awakened to these variously constituted tribes, amid whose creepings, flyings, buzzings, and hummings they have their own being and habitation!

FISHES AND SHELLS.

Again: there are the inhabitants of the waters. It is well known how interesting the distinguished ichthyologist, Agassiz, can make a lecture or an incidental talk about fishes. Both older and younger hang delighted on his descriptions of the finny creatures, hardly thought of before, excepting as now and then seen glancing within their own glassy element, or as presented by quite another sort of professor, — the cook. It is anticipated, that the time will come when parents will be so well informed as to show their children, in table conversation, that trout, haddock, and shad may afford mental as well as bodily nutriment. All that is needed for this purpose is a little reading, observation, and a desire to be instructive.

Some families have on hand a great variety of shells. It would be a pretty exercise for the children, on a winter's day, to sort out these flowers of the sea according to species, size, or some other rule. Thus several of the observing faculties would be cultivated, together with pleasant occupation.

PHENOMENA OF NATURE.

We will glance again at the inanimate world. There are various phenomena and processes in it which may be made interesting and instructive subjects for sight and speech. Nature is passing through changes and performing operations continually all around. The child observes many of them. When they first strike his sense, his curiosity is likely to be aroused; and he may ask, "Why is this or that? what makes it do so?" The loftier reflective faculties are now beginning to operate: they want to know the how, the why, and the wherefore of every thing, especially of the changes and the actions of things. The reflective faculty — the causality more than any other — prompts to questions. In answer to this, the considerate parent will reply and instruct; but many a thoughtless or busy one will turn the child off, and thus stop him from studying lessons and receiving knowledge from the greatest and truest book in the universe, — the universe itself. Before long, in ordinary experience, the child becomes so cu-

tirely accustomed to these natural phenomena, that he loses all curiosity about them, and asks no more questions. Thus millions live and die in the civilized world, and even in this book-blessed and school-favored land, utterly ignorant of wonderful processes going on around them all the time; whereas, had the earliest curiosity been kept up and nurtured, creation would have been an ever-opening and yet untiring volume. I once asked quite a large boy what clouds were made of. He replied, "Smoke." He had seen with his own eyes thick smoke go up into the air from all the chimneys of the neighborhood; and what could it possibly do there but be turned into clouds? Nobody had ever pointed out to him the grand round of the vapors from the ocean and all the waters of the land, up through the sky, and down to the earth, the streams, and the seas again; doing all the world good on the way. Yet that boy was at school, and might have been great at words, remarkable before his school-committee, and wonderful to his parents.

I asked that young girl in the stage-coach, before mentioned, what clouds were; and she replied, "Oh! they are great bags up in the sky; and now and then holes get torn, and down comes the rain." This was all she seemed to know about this ever-varying and manifestly beneficent part of nature. But was she not at a grand boarding-school, learning great words in big books, and at high expense? Was she not getting a fashionable education? What more could the world ask of her?

But it is not boys and girls alone who are ignorant of Nature. A large proportion of the grown-up do not understand her most common operations and appearances. There are mists, clouds, rain, hail, snow, ice, dew, fire, light, air: now, how few in all the civilized world have a philosophical knowledge of these phenomena! Why is it so? One answer may be, that they were not explained to the young. Their eyes, at length, became accustomed to them, the newness passed away, and curiosity passed away with it: so a whole lifetime is spent in ignorance of changes, combinations, and beneficent results, in the wise plans and works of the adorable Creator. Could some such natural phenomenon take place but once in a hundred years, and then be advertised as a spectacle, there would be a rush of eager multitudes to behold it, and a most earnest listening to the scientific explanations. Ah! what minute processes, what mighty move ments, what numberless benefits, every moment! and how millions of the most privileged of our race now live in the midst, and see not, and ask not how or why! Good parents, you are entreated not to suffer your own beloved children to grow up with such deadened curiosity and contented ignorance. If you have not the requisite knowledge already, become fellow-learners with them. A book or two for the purpose can be bought for what you would spend for some transient amusement or perishable luxury.*

The preceding suggestions relate mainly to some of those qualities of objects which together make up their obviously specific character. They have been extended to far greater length, and into much more detail, than was at first anticipated. In consequence of this, there seems to be need of a pause; and here is a convenient place to make it.

---

* The treatises here named would be convenient: Tate's "First Lessons in Philosophy, or Science of Familiar Things;" Wells's "Science of Common Things;" Brewer's "Guide to the Scientific Knowledge of Things Familiar;" and Peterson's "Familiar Science, or the Scientific Explanation of Common Things."

FURTHER SUGGESTIONS

ON

THE DISCIPLINE OF THE OBSERVING FACULTIES.

NOTE.

The following suggestions pertain to a different class of qualities, — those which are not inherent in substance itself, but which are circumstantial and concomitant. These also are exceedingly important subjects of the observing faculties, and afford occasion for careful direction and discipline on the part of parents and other teachers. Those who have an earnest and conscientious interest in early and right mental culture will proceed without requiring any special invitation.

FURTHER SUGGESTIONS.

PLACE.

PLACE, OR GEOGRAPHY AT HOME.

A CHILD may begin geography long before he goes to school, or rather he may lay the sure and proper foundations for this science. When he shall have been taught the points of the compass, — East, West, North, and South; then which side of the room the fire is, which the table, and in which direction are the barn and the garden: and when he shall see just how the land lies and looks, close around his home, — he has had an introduction to geography; or has, in a small degree, been prepared for an introduction. A beginning has been made according to the real nature of things. He understands what he asks about, and what he is told. All the words have a meaning to his little mind. Now, what you may do, and what he will be glad of, is, that you carry him on a little farther and still farther than he would go, clearly and certainly, without your personal guidance. You must talk him along, and walk him along, until you have together surveyed the neighborhood all around, and he has obtained a positive knowledge of it; a knowledge which he feels to be his own, just as he feels that a knowledge of your door-yard or sitting-room is his own. For instance, you can ask him in what direction the street runs; and, if he has not already found out, tell him, and he will soon know beyond forgetting. Have him learn who lives in the next house to his own home, on the right hand and on the left; who, in the second, third, and fourth; and so on. Of course, this could hardly be done in the brick-blocked, heterogeneously neighbored but unneighborly city. Children at a very early age somehow learn what are a road, a field, a pasture, a wood, a hill, and a brook. Indeed, they quickly become familiar with most of the prominent features of nature, and the words by which they are designated. They learn much by the incidental conversation of persons around. But you might, by a little pains, make your child a more accurate as well as far-reaching observer than he would otherwise be. Train him to notice every distinct object within the scope of his eye; all the inequalities of the surface; all the varying tints of the vegetation, between the first tender green of the spring and the russet of the autumn. Every rock, every little hillock and bush, or whatever else may make a distinctly observable thing, should be a lesson to his eye. Were these diminutive traits in the landscape only magnified, they would be such geographical features as might be noticed in the big schoolbook; yet the fact, that they are but insignificant lines and dots as it were, does not make them ungeographical. If geography, according to precise definition, is a description of the earth, — then, when these diminutive things shall be described by your child, he makes real geography out of them; and it will be unspeakably more profitable than the dry, hard descriptions of text-books, as they have generally been forced upon poor little learners, or rather wordgetters. If a child be accustomed to such minute observation, he will not, of course, overlook the more prominent marks in a prospect. But, in further commendation, even some of these minutiæ of the land's surface are important indications to the eye of science; and would you not be glad to have your son look at nature with such an eye? Wherever he shall ramble or travel, would you not have him exercise a keen, detective sight, instead of a vacant gaze?

HOW NOT TO GET LOST.

The exact understanding of the points of the compass is practically of no small importance. Many persons most easily lose the direction, when they find themselves in a new place. Indeed there are those who are absolutely so turned about, that sunrise and sunset seem to have exchanged horizons; and it takes some considerable looking-round and reflection to get out of the bewildering dilemma. Did all roads run at right angles toward East and West, North and South, and were all houses built square upon them, there would be no difficulty. But, transversed and crooked in all directions as roads and streets have to be, the points of compass are sometimes hardly found in a whole lifetime. Indeed there are those who, after a long residence in Boston, scarcely know the direction in which runs that most familiar of all its thoroughfares, Washington Street; or which way exactly the grand and far-seen State House faces. It seems, then, that there might be a real advantage in early and continually training the observation as to the points of the compass. At home, it can be made a matter altogether incidental, and cost no time which may be better employed. Let the cardinal points be well fixed, and it will be easy then to fix in the child's mind the direction of prominent objects between, and also the course of the streets, roads, and streams.

In the exercise of individualizing objects before mentioned, as the child's understanding shall advance, it will be well to locate the various objects, in all directions, in respect to the points of the compass. There might be a little emulous pastime about it, as was recommended before in the culture of the perceptions. Why should not the parents be at the pains of purchasing a compass for this very purpose? It would cost no more than many other things usually provided, but which might equally as well be done without. With this instrument, every point of direction might be exactly established. Thus it would be not only easy, but pleasant and profitable, for children to be trained, as they grow along up, to know the precise point, from home as a centre, of every farm and house in the town: or, if in the city, of every prominent object there. So accustomed would the young learners become to such definite observations, that, as they should travel out to other towns now and then, they would quite readily fall into these exercises; and the turnings of a road or the windings of a stream, the house on a hill, the village-church spire in the distance, might be made an additional trial for this sort of judgment. So eventually, wherever they should travel through the country, their heads would not get confused, as now so often happens. At least, sunrise and sunset would keep their places, to their eye, just as Nature really puts them.

JUDGING OF DISTANCES.

In this connection, it may be well to say something more about the measure of spaces and distances. There is a great deficiency in people's minds generally as to accuracy in distance. One has only to travel in the country, and inquire of various people how far it is from one certain place to another certain place, especially if it be as to the way from one town to another, to be convinced how vague are the notions of many persons in respect to space. Why need this be so, if parents, at odd times, without interfering with any business, should just instruct and amuse themselves and their children in this matter? If a father and son are proceeding to a distant field to work, or to any field, why not for once take a tenfoot pole or a measuring chain, and find out the exact distance? But suppose a boy is going of an errand to a neighbor's, who lives, according to vague supposition, a quarter or half a mile off: let him take his pole or chain, and get the exact measurement, and settle it for good and all. Or, on some leisure time, let the boys, if there are more than one, and the father with them, if he pleases, make a little pastime of the thing. This measuring entertainment may from time to time be extended to any house, or any object, or through any distance whatever, according to convenience. Thus a judgment about distances will be formed, which will come frequently into use in subsequent life.

EDUCATION ON A HILL-TOP.

Suppose, now, a pleasant day, and a little leisure at command, to afford your children, and indeed yourselves equally, some little entertainment,— perchance instruction. You have already become acquainted, it may be, with whatever is within view of home. You have observed every house, field, pasture, wood, rock, shrub, gleam of water. However, it is not necessary to wait to get all these nearest things by eye and heart. Now, take your little company to the highest hill-top you can conveniently reach. From this elevation can be discerned various prominent objects in towns around. Give the young observers the names of these localities, and just the direction in which they lie. There are certain eminences, each perhaps with a name: tell them the name. There, beneath, are the valleys also. Perhaps it may be known, that a considerable river has its course through some of them, or at least some brook large enough to turn the useful mill. Describe these streams, well known to your larger experience, but which the children cannot discern in their sunken and shaded channels. But they can see with the naked eye, as well as you, the many varied features of the landscape between the centre where they stand, and the whole horizon round. Now, make a game of it: see who can count the greatest number of distinct fields or pastures, or separate pieces of woodland, and the greatest number of hills. Indeed, as to this feature, you may let the eye descend to the minutest prominences on the surface, and you will find that the sight will become amazingly sharp, and pick up the least little haycock of a hill at a distance which would not have been thought possible before. Then let the vision hunt after valleys, and any little dips and crinkles in the land's surface, in the same manner. There are cliffs and rocks and single trees standing in open land, and houses and out-houses, to be playfully sought likewise. Withal, take note in which direction exactly any road may run, or valley wind, or stream meander; at what point of the compass any house or hill may be situated. If there shall be a mountain in the distance, there will be something not only to fasten the eye, but to feed it with beauty or lift it to grandeur. Depend upon it, my friends, that you will give your children and yourselves, not only a most entertaining but instructive excursion. The visit to the spot may be repeated several times, before all the objects of the expanse shall fall beneath inspection, or the lesson or the pleasure be exhausted. By and by, you will climb, with your little company of observers, some loftier hill or the mountain-top; and, from such a height, advance your knowledge, possibly, to distant States.

THE USE.

Now, let us consider the practical advantage of this actual observation of the earth's surface, and the various objects, natural or artificial, thereon presented. In the first place, it is evident to all, that the examination of any material thing by the naked faculties is better, for all possible purposes, than the reading or studying of a description of it. It is safer, certainly, to see a farm with one's own eyes before purchasing it, than to trust to any written description. The general who has actually traversed the ground on which he is to make a campaign is far better prepared for its emergencies, than if he knew the field of operations only as presented by the map. The same may be said of every practical concern. The mind must be prepared to comprehend clearly what is distant, and cannot be come at through the naked senses by a thorough inspection of similar things within their reach.

These intellectual facts have scarcely been thought of by parents and teachers generally in this time-consuming, and we may say heart-burdening, matter of education. Now, what do children, for the most part, see when they cast their eyes upon a map? Nothing but a plain surface of paper, with black lines crooking here and there, called roads and rivers; and little dots having the names of towns and cities, with blotches standing for mountains: and this is just about all. The brute animals would take into notice about as much. But with this actual training of the observing powers, as has been recommended, there would appear right on the map, as it were, in definite forms and colors seen by the vivid imagination, real hills, valleys, streams, roads, every thing just as the map was intended to represent them. That plain paper surface would seem moulded into all the various features and appearances of nature by that mind's eye which had been studying the real earth in these pleasant family excursions. Thus geographical language would be all filled, and made rich, with real science,—the earth's facts. Pray, try the experiment, and see.

NUMBER.

WHERE AND HOW ARITHMETIC SHOULD BEGIN.

An early intellectual exercise, as has been before mentioned, is that of individualizing objects; the considering of any separable portion of matter by itself. This idea of distinct things, of individualities, is one of the primitive foundations of all knowledge; and therefore the idea is among the earliest introduced into the mind. This exercise of individuality affords the first occasion for the action of another faculty, — that of number. This, of course, must wait till words can be acquired, and be applied to things. Quite an advance is usually made in a knowledge of things and their names, before the idea of number is distinctly apprehended, and its appropriate terms intelligibly used. Counting, however, is an exercise which children very early perform. Friends put them to it in some playful mood, or to divert them from a trifling grief. They are asked, perhaps, how many thumbs they have, or how many fingers. In this way, or in some other as incidental, that science begins which reaches up into the sublimest mathematics. It does not take long to get through thumbs and fingers, and to the first and all-important waymark, — ten, in the numerical progress. So far, each term has a thing to which it is applied, — a thing to be seen and felt; but, beyond this, the majority of children, according to observation, are taught to use the terms abstractly, — to utter them without any reference to individual and observable objects. There are, no doubt, parents who, in teaching the child, are wise enough to apply, in a much greater extent, the numerals to substantial things. Sometimes children themselves, without any hint from others, will make the application. Nevertheless, the majority, I think, in their first acquisition of numerical terms, are taught the words without things, in the same manner as much of other education is conducted. Now, this need not be so: it ought not to be, inasmuch as individual things are all around, from one up to hundreds, thousands, and millions; and, for every numerical term, there may be a positive object on which to place the eye. Thus the little learner would clearly apprehend, that counting is not merely putting one new word after another, but is adding thing to things, object to objects, one after another: it is making an increase of quantities, under the notice and evidence of his own immediate senses. In counting, for instance, articles of furniture in the room, steps in the stairway, doors and windows in the house, the newly started arithmetical faculty has something real and firm to run along on, as the earlier used perceptive powers have.

In the object-game, recommended in a previous section, there is an excellent opportunity at number: for the game may be not only to see who shall quickest find objects one after another, or who shall come to the very last thing possible to be found, but also who shall come to the largest number including these objects; who shall count the highest in the game. Besides the things in the house, those abroad are sufficient for infinite counting, or until the mind, even of the adult, might get utterly tired and confused in its simple and straight-onward task.

THE COUNTING-GAME.

It is a good plan to train children to observe the proportions between the number and the bulk of things. For instance: it will take about so many apples, or any other kind of fruit, —

considering size, — to fill a certain measure. Let the precise number be ascertained. Make a pleasant thing of the matter; and see who shall come nearest to the fact, in a guess about the measure of fruit from the tree, or of potatoes or turnips or any other production from the ground. Although you make a pastime of your guessing and counting, the judgment thus educated will be a circumstance of positive practical gain in those affairs where gain or loss depends on accuracy of judgment.

This counting-sport might be carried on in many ways, and to an indefinite extent, among brothers and sisters, to enliven the home. But the parents, especially the father, might well, in the evening's leisure, take a part in these numerical operations. Agricultural life affords a great variety of instances for this kind of mental action. Indeed, in any sort of civilized life, there must be purchases of farm-products, and numerous opportunities for maturing the judgment about numbers, quantities, bulk, and, we may add, cost. There is scarcely a family which does not suffer more or less detriment in consequence of poor judgment about commodities bought and moneys paid. Certainly, the needed ability cannot be had, except by experience; and this experience might as well begin as soon as nature gets ready for it, as to be deferred to long afterwards, when immediate occasion shall require.

AN ECONOMICAL IDEA.

One particular application of the numerical faculty is very easy and of practical importance, and must therefore be interesting to the young learner. Various things of household use are in sets, consisting of a definite number. For instance: so many chairs belong to a room; or there is a particular number in a set of crockery, of knives and forks, and of spoons. The child will most easily count these, and hold the number in memory. This is a matter of practical use; for, unless the number of these things is kept in mind, there may be an unheeded loss. It will be really a strengthening of the character, and a positive preparation for carefulness in the future, to give a daughter quite early a specific charge over these more losable implements. There are also other sets of things, the number of which might be obtained and held with advantage; such as napkins, towels, pillow-cases, sheets, and perhaps other kinds of furniture. By this application of the enumerative ability, you might early enlist a daughter's special interest in your goods and their safety. In this connection, moreover, she might be easily led to consider it her duty to keep them all in their proper places, in their proper order, and with all desirable nicety. This care will be a relief to yourself, mother, and a profitable discipline to her.

There is no reason why a boy also might not be trained in this numerical knowledge as to household matters. Of course, he is adequate to it equally with a sister; and, together with her, he is more particularly under the maternal care in his earlier years. It is altogether proper, and it will be beneficial for him, to learn whatever he may, in company and in sympathy with sisters. All indoor knowledge, however minute, will the better qualify him for manhood and a new home of his own. Every man should have at least a general knowledge of his own household affairs, however perfect the wife may be in her administration. Now, inasmuch as a boy's home education ordinarily continues for some years, it would be altogether easy for him to become thoroughly acquainted with the matters belonging to the domestic domain. It could not but be, in most cases, altogether pleasant also, as long as he is privileged with such affectionate companionship.

OUTDOORS.

There are, however, outdoor concerns in which a boy can exercise numerical accuracy and care about sets and classes of things. Let him count the fowls on the premises, get the precise number in each flock of a species, and have an eye that none are missing. So also let him know, and keep in mind, the exact number of cows, sheep, and their young, or whatever else of the domestic animal kind may pertain to the homestead. A sister also might very properly accompany him in sympathy and care; for thus her mind would be expanded, and, without any undue straining or task-work, would easily and agreeably acquire an initiation into that outdoor knowledge which the future wife eventually might wish to have in the possessions, plans, and operations of her husband.

Some may smile at this reference to probable domestic life; but just as surely as early habits of any kind will influence the remote future for good or for evil, so surely will this sort of knowledge and carefulness effect the future economical character of the woman.

OWNERSHIP.

In this counting of furniture sets and of flocks and herds, a child's interest must naturally be quickened by the circumstance, that they belong to parents, and have a certain use. This matter of ownership will draw the little heart toward them. It would be quite a different affair to put the numeric faculty to work on stones in the public road, or pebbles along a water-shore. Let it be especially considered, that the idea of possession and utility will be of no small importance to the incipient arithmetician. In continuing, therefore, this sort of discipline indefinitely onward, let the exercise be as much as possible on objects of property. Let there be a sort of game to see who can recollect the largest number of articles, or sorts of useful things, belonging to the house or the premises around, as they would not all be in immediate sight.

In this thorough enumeration of goods, there is one practical advantage, which is certainly of no small importance. It occasions the young learner to become acquainted in detail with the various commodities, and objects of possession, within and around the home. Young persons generally have but a vague and imperfect knowledge of these things. By this exercise, they will get in mind an inventory of property, almost as if they were making an appraisal. They will acquire a habit of exactness as to what is possessed. Besides, there will come indirectly some notion of the specific uses of things: this will be an additional advantage. How many people have a very confused idea of their own possessions! The confusion reaches and continues into their daily affairs with a quite injurious effect. Now, could an accurate apprehension as to these matters of property be made a habit of the mind from very childhood, it would influence a whole business life. It would certainly be of no small importance in conducting the concerns of a store, especially one containing all sorts of goods, as is more generally the case in the country.

It may be objected to the plan of giving children this special idea of property and ownership, that it will make them think too much of material possessions, and strengthen their affection for these things to a degree which in after-life might be detrimental to the character. Such a consequence would greatly depend on the native mental constitution. No doubt, some children have the love of gain so born with them, that, without any counter-influences, these exercises would really intensify the inherited avarice. But there is to be a moral and religious education; and, if parents are as faithful in this as in the discipline pertaining to material things, any such tendency will, in general, be quite sufficiently counteracted. Let it be understood by readers, once for all, that in this treatise there is intended no such neglect of the higher nature as will leave the lower unrestrained, or in the least degree unbalanced.

COUNTING ON INDEFINITELY.

After the class of things above referred to shall all have been gone over, the exercise may be continued on objects which excite no interest, except that they are to be enumerated one after another, each adding to the sum. With the start which the young numberer gets in the way suggested, he will now be able to count to almost any extent. Let him push ahead on any thing which comes handiest.

Outdoors there are, for lessons, trees in the woods, and stones in the walls. In counting the trees, it may be worth while to remark, there will incidentally arise some knowledge of species and their uses. There must necessarily be caught some glimpses of dendrology, to use a scientific term; which, as long and hard as it seems, a child would remember as well as any other word. Indeed, in touching and individualizing the stones in a wall, as he should trip alongside, what curious varieties he might discover! and thus the diverse riches of mineralogy would now begin to open on him, if not before. Within doors the learner may sit at ease; and with a measure of corn, beans, or peas, or the smaller grains, he may count on for hours, if he shall choose, and renew the operation day after day. And why should he not, if there be time and inducement? He may as well do this at home as many other quite idle things, or something at school called "education," but which amounts to nothing at all toward this end. Every grain he touches is an individual object; it is a unit; it is as much a distinct and observable object as if it were a mountain; it goes to make up a sum which is denominated a thousand or a million. Now, just let a child, of adequate age and ability, enumerate palpable, individual substances in this way; and he will proceed, not vaguely and confusedly, but clearly, definitely, and with a perfect intelligence, to almost any amount of numbers, piled up, in idea, one upon another. Then, when he shall come to the examples of the text-books at school, what otherwise would be empty abstractions will to imagination cover and contain, as it were, like clothing, substantial and definite forms. He will have a distinct idea of numerical quantities and relations, such as will be of invaluable service in the higher mathematical regions, where, as things have been, learners too often grope in a dark and cold misty expanse.

POWER OF CONCENTRATION AND OF INDIVIDUALITY IMPROVED.

Still other benefits from our enumerative exercise may be adduced. It affords opportunity for concentrating attention. It would have the effect to bring a naturally unsteady and wandering mind to act for a time continuously in a specific direction. This is no small matter in education, and also in the practical affairs of life.

Again: the act of counting one by one necessarily develops, more or less, the individualizing faculty. An object must be apprehended as a distinct unit: it is individualized. Perhaps, indeed, this is the best method possible of deve-

loping the central and leading perceptive power.
The occasion would be of special importance to
a child whose individuality might be naturally
weak, as is often the case. Such a person, in
passing along a village street, would have a
vague idea of houses; and this would be all:
but, if he was set to counting the houses, each
one would come, at least momentarily, into distinct notice, and in some degree also its concomitant circumstances. Or, supposing you take
such a child to a store, you might suggest to
him to count, while you are doing an errand, all
the kinds of things he might see on the counter,
shelves, or anywhere else, without being obtrusive beyond propriety. Then afterward, let him
give you his account, and you will find that his
store-visit has been quite an instructive occasion. Still further, the subordinate observing
faculties would be called into exercise more or
less in connection with individuality. Of course,
as each object is enumerated and noticed, its
form, size, color, place, &c., would be also in
some degree observed. Thus we perceive how
a simple operation, which at home is carried
scarcely beyond thumbs and fingers, except in
abstract words, and which is pursued at school
probably never beyond the numerical balls, may

be made the means of large, various, and most profitable discipline.

It is hoped that enough has been said to show clearly, that simple counting is no unimportant item in intellectual discipline. Let it not, then, be neglected because it is not included, to the extent indicated, in the customary educational programme, or because there is no precedent for it in ordinary experience.

BUSINESS ARITHMETIC.

In the young learner's first arithmetical exercise, — enumeration, — the importance of having things to accompany words must be most evident to the reader. But, furthermore, the same will hold true of other numerical operations. The purpose of the ordinary arithmetical education is to prepare the student for the business of adult life. The more, therefore, that numbers and figures directly pertain to real substances and to actual transactions, the more immediate and practical will be their bearing on future exigencies. Could exercises in addition, subtraction, multiplication, division, &c., directly concern commodities; and could they, moreover, be performed right in their midst, — there would be a reality and an interest which could not be felt at the distance of the school, and especially in such abstract examples as generally make the lessons of the book. It is a common remark with business-men, that they did not understand arithmetic, after all the time spent on it at school, till they had occasion to use it in their own actual affairs. The reason of this is very plain. In their business, there are certain material substances. If these are not, at the moment, within sight, they are before the mind's eye: the numerical relations of these things are, therefore, more distinctly apprehended. There is no blur of abstraction about them. A calculation must be made, and this with perfect accuracy: no guesswork can be allowed here. Hence there is a real and pressing demand on the science of number. The interests, the feelings, and the arithmetical operation, all tend together toward one end. Something of immediate and practical importance is to be accomplished. No wonder, then, that men who have quite forgotten their schoolbook rules, should now invent rules of their own; and, as is sometimes the case, even make short cross-cuts to accurate and provable conclusions. Such is the testimony of practical experience.

Now, could instruction be transferred to the

store, the mechanic's shop, or the farm, there is no doubt that arithmetic would be understood and appreciated to a degree which cannot possibly be realized at the schoolroom, as the science is there more generally communicated. The intellect may be, to some degree, disciplined by the abstract lessons there: they are better than nothing. This discipline, however, falls far short of what would come from the demands of actual business.

FAMILY CIPHERING.

But the school must remain in its one assigned location. Its exercises are likely to continue for some considerable time as before, — abstract and unreal; for it takes a long while to improve text-books, and, we may add, to improve some of the teachers who superintend their use. Now, parents, must your children be limited to schoolbook examples? Must they remain with this hazy, half-way knowledge of arithmetic, until they also shall come into the actual business of adult life, or at least that of apprenticeship? By no means, if you will only take a little pains yourselves. You have had your own schooldays, and have gone through the abstractions as your children are doing now, and probably with no more profit. But, since then, you have been putting these dimly apprehended abstractions to concrete and positive use. Perhaps you have been inventing rules and methods of your own. At any rate, you can apply number and figure to visible and palpable commodities, to all the intents and purposes of livelihood and accumulation. Now, it is just such an application which your own children need at this very moment, and which most probably they cannot have, except in an imperfect degree, at school. Why, then, shall they not have it at home, and under the instruction of those whom they naturally love better than any one outside the family circle? All you have to do is to sit down among them in the leisure evening, and present the examples of your own business, just such as you have worked out in your own head, or on slate or paper, at your need. If you have been long in life, your memory must abound in instances; or you can invent numerous examples similar to what really occur. Depend upon it, arithmetic will put on a new aspect to the learners, all the brighter and all the more pleasant because it shines out from a light reflected by the most beloved and trusted friends. If you have not been called by your own affairs to make much use of numbers, and your own school-abstractions — figure-shadows, as they may be called — have been quite forgotten, have fallen even from shadows into absolute nothingness, — then you can become a fellow-learner with your children. With this fresh school-knowledge, such as it is, they can perhaps instruct you, or at least be the occasion of your learning. You can, at least, mutually assist each other in real, lifelike performances in calculation. Your larger general experience and maturer judgment will, of course, take a respected lead. Home is the proper place for children in the evening; but then there must be work or study, or some sort of entertainment, to make home agreeable, and worth staying in, preferably to any outside allurements. Suppose, now, for once you try, among other things, this arithmetical experiment; and see if it does not, as the saying is, come to something.

EXPLANATION.

By what has been said, let it not be inferred that any objection is intended to the more abstract exercises in numbers, in due process of an advanced education. This right beginning indicates really no hinderance to an ascent into the veriest sublime of mathematics. Indeed, the best assurance for the profoundest attainments in this science must be thoroughly distinct ideas of material objects in their numerical relations at the outset.

In conclusion, let me say that I have dwelt to such extent on this topic, for the reason, that, in the arithmetical branch of education, as in almost every other, time, pains, and money are spent out of all proportion to profitable results. Boys and girls, instead of going straight on, step after step, in clear light and on a palpable path, learning the world and its things as they really are, wander, or rather perhaps are driven, over ground without any certain foot-hold, — a sort of ghost-land. They are set to peer after and strike at flitting images, and not to lay hold on substantial knowledge, which stops and stays in the hand.

ACTION.

THE POWER OF EVENTUALITY.

It is one of the earliest perceptive functions to observe action, to see what things do, to watch curiously for what shall be done next. No matter what it is that acts or simply moves: the little eyes are intent. It may be the flitting of a feather or the flutter of a leaf. If the object is a living one, like the kitten, the dog, the horse, or a bird, how delightedly the varying movements are followed! The comings and goings of human beings still more strike attention, especially those of new forms and faces, which may happen along.

Now, the observing of movement requires a distinct operation of the intellect. Puss asleep and perfectly still in her corner is a subject of notice altogether different from her skipping across the room and hopping into some indulgent lap. So different is the action of an individual object from the individual itself, that phrenologists affirm there must be a distinct faculty to take cognizance of it. Indeed, they think they have discovered a special organ for the purpose in the brain. This organ, the physical and material together, is denominated Eventuality. Whether the theory be true or not, it gives us a more distinct idea of the intellect in its relation both to actions in continuance and actions completed. Now, this particular observing faculty is of incalculable importance in the educational course of the young. It needs a systematic and thorough discipline as much as any other power.

DIFFERENCES IN THE OBSERVING POWER.

Parents and educators have scarcely thought of the difference between one person and another as to the ability of clearly perceiving actions as they occur before the sight. Even in the same family, one organization will be found much superior to another as to this sharp-sightedness at events. One particular child will be strangely and habitually unobservant of incidents around. Ask him if he saw such a thing done, and he knows nothing about it. It is as if he had been closed round with a thick mist, or been living in a dream-world of his own, or had no eyes at all. His brother, much younger it may be, catches, at the same time, every passing circumstance as with a kind of appetite. He will look and learn at any rate. He will see incidents just in the order and connection in which they took place, and he will narrate them with equal exactness. Now, these differences will run on through life, and characterize the mental operations and acquirements, and perhaps the material fortunes, of the two relatives. The originally strong power will become stronger through ever-new occasions, which it instinctively seizes on just for its own gratification. It will grow because it cannot help growing. On the other hand, the defective perception will still continue weak and inadequate; that is, unless it shall be developed by special training or by peculiar circumstances of business or necessity.

The eventuality of the majority of people, though of normal and average strength, is so utterly neglected in specific education as but very imperfectly to perform its office. The world is full of action. Things inanimate are in movement, and produce effects. Living creatures, while awake, are almost always in casual motion, or in definite procedure to certain ends. So thick, so various, are activities of one sort and another around the human being, that he cannot possibly notice all of them. He observes only a part, and such as attendant circumstances may bring to sight. Even these he may not observe distinctly and accurately, because there seems no special need of it. He notices, if he notices at all, simply because he happens to look. As a general matter, there is no directness of attention caused by any previous special discipline. There is, moreover, no sense of moral obligation through which he shall endeavor to know exactly what takes place as he looks. Of course, if there is no call for particularity, why should the child or the youth be particular? He will have no more reason for it than he would have in counting the trees in the orchard, or the stones in the wall, till he should be put upon the exercise, as in the case of the arithmetical discipline which has been already advised.

CONSEQUENCES OF NEGLECTED CULTURE.

Thus it is that a faculty of incalculable practical importance has failed in its office; and, like all neglects and failures, this has been followed by more or less of retribution. To consider all the evils resulting from inaccurate observation of facts, and careless statements about them, would be to take in all the world and all time since Adam's fall. Words and figures would fail of the amount. A few instances will give us some faint idea of the abounding evil.

A careless young observer, giving an account of some disorder in a schoolroom, will make a statement quite different from what might have come from another witness with a clear-seeing eye. In consequence, some poor urchin may get an unjust punishment. The same careless describer of the offence, coming to be a man, or even before he arrives at this age, may be called to the witness-stand in a court of justice; and may unintentionally testify so wide of the truth as to what his eyes seemed to behold, that a fellow-man may innocently be subjected to fine, imprisonment, or even death on the gallows. Now, consider all the millions of cases, which, in all the world, have been brought before magistracies and juries, and there decided according to testimony; and we can have some idea of the thousands of unjust decisions, — unjust because of the imperfect perceptions of really honest witnesses.

Take human society as it exists everywhere around us. Suppose any city, town, village, or even little neighborhood: what misapprehensions and misstatements of facts are continually occurring! Now and then, some base scandal starts up, and comes to an enormous growth. In the majority of such cases, the story is not an entire fabrication. There has been some incident as a groundwork. But the eyes of the first observer and reporter of that incident were so inadequate to their office, that he gave only a part of the truth, or added a trifle to it. Thus the error first sprang into existence; then, passing from lip to lip, it grew at length into a great fiction, having but little of the original verity about it. All this might happen through a mere intellectual defect, without the least intention of departure from the exact truth.

Again: the mistake might originate from the same incapacity in some one of the hearers of an affair. It must be understood, that those persons, who would naturally see a transaction but imperfectly, would also, from the same weakness of faculty, get imperfect notions in hearing an account of a transaction, even if that should be thoroughly correct. In the first place, they receive but a dim idea of an occurrence as it comes to the ear; then they but faintly remember it. In a procedure embracing a series of incidents, some one item or more may fall out of memory altogether. Consequently, their statement of the case will make quite a different matter. Thus, however exactly truthful a first observer and narrator may be, hearers will inadvertently receive only dim and altogether inadequate ideas of an affair. In this way, a chance auditor of some truthful narration may start a most egregious error on its irrepressible course through the lips and ears of a community. While there is but one original witness, and he entirely truthful, there may be at length a hundred hearers of his account, many of whom will unintentionally repeat it with more or less variation from the facts as they come to their ears. No wonder that falsifications so numerously and so universally prevail, when we consider this one simple, unthought-of intellectual deficiency.

Still, all the evil is not to be imputed to this source. There are very often moral perversities through which such mistakes are magnified, and made far more operative for evil. A characteristic love for gossip, together with peculiar imaginative ability, will enlarge a trifle into wonderful magnitude, and diversify it with curious forms. But, what is much worse, an uncharitable, sensorious disposition will exaggerate and blacken little innocent affairs into heinous sins or even enormous crimes. A bad spirit, with a big imagination, will create monsters out of almost nothing. Thus it is that heartburnings, broken friendships, and even bloody assaults and cruel murders, have come to pass without number. Very few, as society has been and now is, go through life without some personal experience of the sort.

MISTAKEN SUBMISSION TO THE EVIL.

Such carelessness has there always been in observation and statement, so uncommon is perfect accuracy, that errors are taken as a matter of course, and as what cannot be helped. While an individual is under personal grievance, he will complain of careless eyes and truthless speech; but otherwise there is a singular indifference to the evil. People do not expect the truth. They are inured to falsehood, and let it go. No idea of improvement in the way of education has occurred probably to one in a thousand. Any moral obliquity, it is expected, may possibly be corrected by Christian influences; but any thing further is hardly considered within the range of reform. Things are as they have been; and so must they continue to be, unless supernatural influences shall arrest their course, and make a change.

WHAT A NEW DISCIPLINE WOULD DO.

It is rational to suppose, that much improvement may be achieved by simply understanding the mental organism, and conforming the early discipline to its conditions. There is a great advantage in good intellectual habits, independent of moral convictions and principles, if these latter influences on conduct cannot be had. Let a child be trained, as a matter of discipline, to see and describe things exactly as they are; and this habit of accuracy will continue in after-life, just as any other habit may continue, entirely separate from the thought of moral obligation. A person may be educated to extraordinary facility in arithmetical calculations: no moral element enters into this peculiar ability. Just so it may be with the perception of events. Could all the families of a neighborhood be trained, from their earliest infancy upward, to see things precisely as they are, and to describe them just as they were seen; and could the same discipline be carried into schools, and the pupils there be trained to be as exact in observation and description as they are trained to be exact in performing arithmetical problems, — there would be an unexampled improvement in conversational trustworthiness and in neighborly relations. There would be, as there is in other things, a sort of emulative desire for accuracy, and perfect truthfulness to fact. A failure as to the precise fact would lower the intellectual standing and reputation. A faulty observer and teller of incidents would be considered as poorly educated, like a blundering reader or a bad speller. Could such a discipline be carried into every family and every school of the country, there would be a national reform. A whole people would be educated to see events accurately, as they might be educated to survey correctly and minutely the geographical features of their native town, as was recommended in the suggestions about place. They would be capacitated not only to observe actions in their progress, but to apprehend the causes and the results of action to a degree beyond all former precedent. Could moral and religious motives be brought to bear on this point of culture as they ought, what wonders of improvement might be accomplished! But the all-important aid of the conscience and the heart will be hereafter considered.

HOW THE DISCIPLINE MAY BEGIN.

As soon as a child shall be able to tell his experiences, it may easily be perceived what native strength and precision of eventuality he may possess. Then, according to his lack must be the particularity and assiduousness of his educators.

Now the question comes, Where and how shall the necessary training be commenced? There need be no search after lessons; for — to use several of the appropriate terms — motion, action, incidents, events, and facts are close by, and everywhere around. The first thing that happens may be an exercise of discipline, if the child is old enough to notice and give some account of it. Still there must be advantage in system; and, for this reason, one subject will be preferable to another.

Certain transactions are better suited to begin with than others, which might be good for a further stage of progress. It is one of the acknowledged rules of education to commence with what is best known or can be most easily known, and thence proceed to things more difficult. The chief requisites are distinctness of perception, and correctness in recital. It is important that the several parts of a proceeding should be noticed according to their precise succession. Those operations are excellent for attention and questioning, at the outset, in which first one thing is done, then another, in necessary order.

HOUSEHOLD LESSONS.

The industrial concerns of a household are numerous and diverse: let them by turns become lessons for observation. No better instances can be presented to children than the goings-on around them in ordinary work. They are interested in what their friends do. The smiling aspect and kind tones of invitation will be all that is wanted to enlist their special attention to any movement, or series of movements, performed by their domestic friends.

But let us illustrate. Take, for example, the setting of the table for dinner. There is, first, the drawing-out of the table to the proper position; second, the lifting and fastening of the leaves; then the spreading of the cloth; and so on, — one performance after another, till the meal is ready, and the family are at knife and fork. Now, let the child, as a matter of discipline, exactly describe every process of the table-setting in its exact order. Let there be no mistake in the sequences, as perfect accuracy in this particular respect is one of the benefits of the lesson. The same use may be made of other household duties in which there is a methodical routine. Of course, children, whether desired or not, usually notice these proceedings. These are among the occasions of that unconscious and gradual development of intellect which will go on without care or thought on the part of the little lookers or their friends. But, according to their native power of eventuality, they may notice each particular of a transaction in its due order, or they may have but imperfect perceptions and confused ideas. The important point aimed at is accuracy in seeing and telling, as a settled characteristic; an ability which shall prevent no small harm, and do great good, in that future which depends so much on early formed habits. Take mental constitutions as they average, and this perfect exactness of sight and speech cannot be had without some special discipline. The practical advantages warrant all the pains which can possibly be given to the subject.

MANUFACTURING LESSONS.

Besides the various kinds of orderly work at home, the several divisions of skilled labor, the distinct and life-long occupations of people, will afford most valuable exercises in this sort of observation.

First, take those more simple mechanical trades which are common in every country village or town, and are mainly carried on by hand. In each one of these, there is an orderly procedure: first, one thing is done; then, another; and so on through a course of work. Now, let a child of adequate age watch the processes, and afterward give an exact account. In due time, have him visit mills and factories, and trace their more complex operations; noticing how the several connected forces produce results.

AGRICULTURAL LESSONS.

Educational visits to the farm must certainly not be omitted. Its affairs are probably more numerous and diverse than those of any other separate productive employment. From the first touch of culture in the spring till all the harvests are gathered in, there is orderly, progressive work. Then, in the winter, there is the kindly care of animals in several daily processes. There are, besides, useful but less regular doings which come in between the rest. Now, all these matters, judiciously presented, would be exceedingly interesting and instructive to the fresh perceptions of the young. They should begin their agricultural observations with the earliest movements in the spring. Let them notice every distinct kind of labor in all its items, and these in their orderly and precise succession. Then an account should be required as perfectly exact as any prescribed recitation at school.

BENEFITS.

All industrial occupations might afford lessons similar to those indicated above. It is not necessary to particularize any farther. Now, it cannot be doubted, that this peculiar discipline would be of inestimable advantage to the young as candidates for life's activities and uses. No descriptive books could equal, or make up for, this positive knowledge caught by the naked eye.

One ·special and important benefit would be the obtaining of some considerable insight into the various trades and pursuits of men. The pupil would also learn something, not only about methods of procedure, but about the materials and implements used. What is, moreover, of much consequence, he would obtain that knowledge of different kinds of business which is really necessary to develop his own taste, and to form his judgment in respect to the choice of an employment for himself. Still further, he would eventually come to that understanding of the various avocations of men which is quite necessary to form a just estimate of their respective and peculiar services. Indeed, such a knowledge would lead to that charity and kindliness which is so much needed, but is so often withheld.

WHAT A FATHER MIGHT DO.

It may be averred, that, in this intelligent part of the country, most people have some general ideas of the different departments of industry. But why not possess a more thorough and systematic knowledge, when it can be so easily gained? During the years usually devoted to education, there might be obtained a quite extensive and comparatively intimate acquaintance with the various pursuits of life, and this without much that would seem like a task. Nothing would be necessary but simply to take or make occasions. A father could scarcely better employ a little respite from business, than to take his children, as a pleasant pastime, to places of various industrial activity. A small portion of the time now spent in school on studies unadapted to the pupil's age, but faintly understood and quickly forgotten, would suffice for the purpose.

NATURE'S WORKS AND WAYS.

Man's art and industry should not engage the whole attention. In the mean time, let children, from the earliest ability, observe the movements and processes of nature. If they are capable of admiring human inventions and their effects, they can be led to admire and study the wonderful machinery by which the Creator brings about results. Some will see and reflect considerably, and ask questions, and grow in knowledge with but little prompting. It is not so with the majority. They soon become so accustomed to all regular phenomena, that they cease to think much about them. As for the more covert processes, excepting such as may unexpectedly startle their sight, they scarcely, by themselves alone, find them out. Whatever is going on continually in regular successions of movement, and which has been thus going on from the earliest remembrance, is unheeded by most, simply because of this very order and constancy. It is with people, as they grow gradually up, in respect to the mechanism of nature, as it is in respect to the household timepiece: they are so accustomed to its tick, tick, that they do not hear it; and, if they happen to catch a glimpse of the inner machinery, they have no curiosity to study a structure, which, close by, has served their convenience so well and so long.

These faculties, thus admirably fitted to observe and know, should not become so deadened and useless. The infinite Designer and Maker did not so intend. The infant possessor begins early and aright to use them. His innate instincts, almost as soon as he fairly gets his eyes open, prompt him to look and learn. How intently he gazes on the flickering flame or the waving tree! He is pleased with any sort of gentle motion. But these instincts should grow into earnest desires to look farther and farther, and to learn still more and more. All that is needed with most is easily-given direction and sympathy. At first, the child simply observes movement, and has no thought beyond the impression on his sight. But this observation is the initiative step toward the whole philosophy of causes, effects, and uses. This one perceptive power, eventuality, holds the key, as it were, to all natural science. This science, in large degree, consists in understanding how the masses and elements of matter, and the organic forms of it, act on each other, and what are the ends designed. Of course, the action must first be known before it can be discerned whence it comes, or to what it tends. What rounds, and ranges, and mazes of movement between the stupendous rolling and circling of worlds and the leaping affinities of atoms!—an infinitude of agents and activities; millions of distinct organs and offices and operations, yet one connected and harmonious mechanism, moved every moment by one infinite Power. Now, parent, shall all this be no more to your beloved child's curiosity than the everswinging pendulum or the ceaseless tick of the old, convenient clock?

CASUAL EVENTS.

Besides those processes which take place in regular routine, and which may be repeatedly observed by the learner, and, as it were, got by heart, there are other occurrences which are fortuitous and unexpected. Nothing before has been exactly like them, and nothing will follow exactly similar in the collocation of all the several objects and circumstances. Events of this sort are transpiring every moment. Mankind, exercising their own wills, are continually doing this and that, according to contingencies. It is such transactions, not distinctly observed, and affording no second opportunity for better sight, which occasion those misstatements whence come innumerable difficulties and heart-burnings in society. Perfect accuracy, in observing and representing these, is of surpassing importance. A habit of being truthful to facts should as early as possible be formed. To this end, no discipline can hardly be too persistent and thorough.

Those unimportant incidents, ever new and various, which are continually happening within and around the home, present the most convenient lessons to the little observer. Of course, it is not necessary that he shall get through all the methodical processes before alluded to, even those within the house, before he may be put upon these. Let it be an emphatic requirement, that, in his account, he shall omit no circumstance, nor put one out of its exact order, any more than he did in the case of the table-setting, or any other fixed and regular proceeding. Thus a habit will be formed of distinct and consecutive observation. Besides, in this way, the young mind will be aided in acquiring that ability of concentrated attention which is so important to success in either study or business.

If those casual occurrences which are in themselves of no special importance shall be accurately noticed, those transactions which make their mark on a day or a week, or on the times, will, of course, secure the pupil's close and minute attention. There are those proceedings which may be not only a discipline, but a rich instruction. Among these are public movements and spectacles. Some of them grow out of prevalent tastes and customs; such as funeral and civic processions, ordinary military parades, and anniversary occasions. Others make a part of the history of the times; such as the marching of troops and the sailing of war-vessels, as in the present great national crisis. Hitherto, no specific and circumstantial attention to such events has generally been required as a part of education; but they afford lessons of far greater value, if rightly conducted, than are found in the naked, crumb-like facts of some historical text-books, which wearily occupy much time in seminaries of learning.

INFLUENCE UPON LITERATURE.

It is by no means intended to disparage the study of well-written history. Indeed, this intent and thorough observation, this study of passing affairs, will be a valuable preparative for the study of history in the school, or for the profitable perusal of it at any subsequent time. It will be a useful qualification for any sort of reading in which facts are comprised. A person who, from constitutional defect, takes but a slight or confused notice of present occurrences, will have but a slight remembrance of them. He will have a much more imperfect idea and remembrance of transactions which are presented only through language. The action-noting faculty, which has been well disciplined by what transpires immediately before it, will be more readily impressed by mere verbal communications. A narrated occurrence will thus be more clearly conceived of: it will not seem distant and dim, but, as it were, present and distinct, to this particular observing power. The memory, moreover, will be proportionally retentive; for each intellectual faculty is supposed to have a memory of its own, so that the eventuality which is keen to perceive is also strong to retain.

This exactness in the knowledge and presentation of events, as a matter of culture and general habit, must necessarily have a most salutary effect upon the literature of the people, both that which they themselves make and that which is made for them. If conversation shall become more true to fact, epistolary communications will share the improvement. Gossip by the pen will be reformed as well as gossip by the tongue. But, beyond this, historical compositions will be characterized by more thorough and satisfactory research. A public opinion which has been trained up to the mark of absolute truth must press upon the responsibility of writers, so that history, in future, shall not have to be rewritten, and the characters of men rejudged, as heretofore, for the sake of right and justice.

Again: with this better culture as to action, fictitious productions, which now make so large a part of the common reading, will be altogether more faithful to nature. No small portion of the novels, and especially of the juvenile tales, of the day, are poor representations of human life.

Their authors seem to have been living, from childhood up, in an imaginary world. They have not studied, as they should, nature and man, in those multitudinous activities by which traits and qualities are truly made known. Now, this special culture of eventuality will supply fancy and invention with those truthful materials which have hitherto been so much wanting. Thus the creations of genius will become verisimilitudes of what has been actually experienced, or what at least is possible to man in view of the known principles of his being and his surrounding conditions.

Coming generations will have this true literature. When the whole people shall be trained to an exact observation of the real and moving world, then the few who shall write for the people will not fail of that best discipline and knowledge which comes through the primitive and surest use of the eyes.

NEWSPAPER REFORM.

One of the most important benefits to come from eventuality, as it should be, is the improvement in newspaper literature. Everybody in our country, who can read at all, reads the newspaper. It exerts a wider and deeper influence than any other emanation from the press. It does unmeasured good, but also much evil. A new appetite has been engendered, or rather a constitutional one intensified tenfold. It is a rabid hunger for something new; and, besides this, for something as much as possible exciting. The newspaper would not be a newspaper unless it furnished this new thing. Hence a competition between journals. That goes off best which contains the keenest stimulative for the moment. The slightest rumor is caught up, and made the most of to-day; but it may be utterly contradicted to-morrow. No matter: it serves its end; it satifies the craving. Thus, if no other harm is done, thought is prevented from settling down on serious and really important subjects. The popular mind is unsettled, and is kept unsettled and unstable. There is especially a bad effect upon the young, who, as they grow up, ought to be getting their faculties more and more, and continually, into a condition of strength and consolidation. For thorough-going, substantial reading, there is not time; and as for deeper science and philosophy, they are scarcely thought of after leaving the school.

Now, should there be an education from the earliest to a clear perception of passing incidents, and to a thoroughly accurate statement of them, the young would come up into life with a habit of accuracy, and, in consequence, with a taste for it. Vague observation, and more vague description, would be no part of their experience. For such readers, the newspaper item about somebody or something must have a ground of probability. If such things shall be found within a day or a week utterly false, the public taste and habit will say, "Away with them! nothing of this!" Thus journals will compete with each other for exactness to the truth. A public man's character will have a safety not recently experienced. A distinguished lady's delicacy will not be offended by some false rumor about her, as is now sometimes the case, published from end to end of the land. Thousands of things, utterly unwarranted, will not be breathed into growth, as at present, by this hot breath of desire for the new and exciting.

In this advanced age, when steam and telegraph bring news from all quarters of the world, sufficient for every day's entertainment, falsehood will not be needed. Indeed, there will hardly be leisure to glance along the abundance of authenticated facts; and many of these, in this new and wonder-producing era, may be quite as attractive to curiosity as any catch-penny fabrications, or even the more innocent scintillations of genius.

PARTISAN CALUMNIES CHECKED.

But, above all, the bitter calumnies of political partisanship must receive a wholesome check, if they do not utterly come to an end. These are the worst concomitants of our elective government. These are the abominations of the country. These too often thrust our best men prematurely into retirement, or prevent them from coming out of it at all. As things are now, character is mangled, murdered, in political warfare. Could the people of this country be trained to be faithful to fact, a salutary influence must be exerted in this direction. A change for the better would be wrought, such as hitherto has never been known in popular governments. If absolute fact be demanded, all electioneering misrepresentations must cease. That party which should resort to falsifications must succumb; must wear written on its very forehead, *Wrong*. Let a thorough examination into facts be the groundwork of political opinion, and the reason, the intelligence, the common sense, of voters would bring an overwhelming majority to the side of the right and the best. The people would come to know who are their truly wise, good, and great men, and would give to them their confidence. The people would confide also in each other. Then, instead of democracy, deceived, cheated, degraded, and made a byword through the monarchies of Europe, there would be a democracy like the clear shining of the sun after the rain, enlightening the eyes, and warming the hearts, of the common masses all over the world. It would be like a great luminary in the heavens, ascending towards its noon, it might be, but there to stand still, as the sun did of old, while the true and the faithful everywhere should become victorious and free.

PRESENT STATE OF OUR NATION.

But such a state of things has not yet been, and many fear that it will not exist perhaps for ages. Our nation, at this moment, heaves and tosses like ocean in the storm; yea, as with the more terrible earthquake, opening new chasms downward, shooting new volcanoes upward, even shaking the nations that are afar off, and perplexing monarchs on their thrones. And all this has come from the lies of selfish, wicked men. Old custom, the love of ease, of power, of wealth, and luxury, could not possibly have prevailed, had it not been for this diabolical "refuge of lies." Had the truth as to facts, nothing but the truth, been presented from the platform and the press for the last thirty years; had the people received the truth, and reflected it to each other just as the millions of the summer dew-drops reflect the unfailing, benignant sun,— the present fratricidal war could never have been. It would have been as utterly impossible as for hailstones and thunderbolts to have fallen from the cloudless sky on herb and beast and man below.

The demons of falsehood still divide the land. The father of lies himself hangs, as it were, invisibly over it, in all his hideous, heaven-defying malignity, and scatters his own arrows of destruction into the ears and the understandings and down into the hearts of a credulous people. What the end will be, no one but the omniscient God, or foreseeing and truthful angels, can tell. Parents, teachers! such now is the state of our country; and why is it so, why has it been so? Because the parents and teachers, your predecessors, generation back behind generation, did not train the young to see the truth, to speak the truth, and to live the truth. It is because the educators themselves have been false: how, then, could they train their children and pupils to be true?

Now, shall this state of things remain? Shall it be ages before we shall be a stable people, with a stable government and a stable prosperity? It all depends upon you, parents and teachers of this nation, whether we shall grow into safety, and realize the hopes of yearning millions the earth over, or not. Accept the views which have been here imperfectly presented as to training to the truth; let them be adopted in the family, in the school, in the land throughout; and, with one addition in the educational plan, there will be, there must be, inevitable success.

DISCIPLINE OF THE CONSCIENCE.

But this addition is the most important matter of all. Without it, there can be no assurance of steady progress and of final security. This is the culture of the conscience, side by side, with the discipline of the observing intellect. Nothing can be more true, as all history proves, than that the human heart is deceitful above all things, and desperately wicked. Such is the selfishness of human nature, — a selfishness acting from very infancy, and strengthening with the years, subjugating the intellect to its service, — that the conscience must be awakened at the earliest, and set to its restraining work. All the solemn warnings of religion will be needed with some constitutions to make the tongue's statement true to the eye's witnessing. Parents, upon you is imposed, by the infinitely True, the responsibility of quickening the moral sense of your children to the surest guardianship over the tongue, and, indeed, over the feelings and motives which lie beneath the speech. Teach them, that knowingly to deviate from exactness, even as to trivial incidents, is to be guilty of falsehood, and falsehood replete with danger; for it prepares the way for more serious deviations, and thence more heinous obliquity. Impress upon them, that what has once really taken place is fixed: it has been, it exists as a fact for ever. However human beings may misconceive it, take from it, or add to it, there it is, printed on the irreversible page of the past; there it is, moreover, naked before the Omniscient Eye. Neither wishes nor prejudices nor passions, nor volumes of words, can change it one tittle. In the process of time, and in the passing-away of temporary motives and feelings, events may come to be seen in their true light. Then self-seekers and falsifiers will stand out exposed in the same light, and in their naked deformity. Train your children, therefore, to believe and to feel that they might as well struggle up, despite of gravitation, into the clouds for a hiding-place, as to struggle away, and for ever keep away, from the fastness of fact and the searching severity of truth.

TWO BEINGS WHO CANNOT BE ESCAPED.

There are two beings from whom the untruthful man cannot conceal his guilt. One is himself. At the moment of its utterance, he is conscious of the falsehood. Henceforth it is written on his memory that he has *lied*. He can no more wipe it out than he can wipe out the wrinkles on his brow above it, or shape into infantile openness the sinister expression of his face. There it is, registered on his memory for ever. It may sink away from the constant glance of his own thought, perhaps it may remain unseen for years; but it is not gone. The leaves of more recent experiences are but laid over it. Some time, with lightning swiftness, those leaves may be flung back; and *there*, as in years long before, blazes out the record,—*falsifier*, *liar*. Teach your children, therefore, that, if the untruthful shall escape all the rest of the world, he shall ever, ever, be pursued and found by HIMSELF.

The other being from whom the liar cannot hide is that One of whom it is said in the sacred oracles, "He that planted the ear, shall he not hear? He that formed the eye, shall he not see? Shall not God search this out? For his eyes are upon the ways of man, and he seeth all his goings. There is no darkness, nor shadow of death, where the workers of iniquity may hide themselves. Hell and destruction are before the Lord: how much more, then, the hearts of the children of men!"

TIME.

In close connection with action is another important matter of discipline. It regards the relation of time. Movement occupies more or less of duration according to the space or distance passed through, or according to the number of motions, as in those indicated by the ticking of a time-piece or in the pulsations of the blood. It is supposed that there is a special faculty for the perception of time, as there is in the case of other qualities and relations in nature. There are those who can tell almost any hour of the day or night, without clock or watch. Such persons have a naturally keen perception of time, which has been increased by constant use. They are always to a moment punctual to their engagements. They keep nobody waiting; that is, if their moral nature is as true as their one intellectual ability. Others have a character directly the reverse. Owing to a constitutional weakness, or the undeveloped condition of this faculty, they have but little consciousness of the passing moments. In early life, they are behind at school, unless well prompted: as they grow up, they are behindhand in their engagements, behind in their business, behind at public meetings. Are they on committees or in any service associated with others: they are always tardy, and keep their fellow-officials in uneasy endurance. Perhaps, when they do arrive, they may consume much time in needless talk, through the same unconsciousness which made them late.

TIME IN TALK.

Some persons are particularly unconscious of time in conversation. They will spend the whole space allotted to the call of a friend on some casual topic uninteresting and tedious to the hearer, who may wish to touch on subjects more accordant with his tastes, or on which he came especially to confer. Cases are not infrequent, in which speakers, who had been appointed together with others to address an audience, have appropriated to themselves nearly the whole time of the occasion. An opening speech has been known to consume about the whole evening.

PUBLIC OCCASIONS.

Again: how often are the movements of various public occasions tediously delayed by the few persons, and indeed by some one individual, having the direction! So common are such delays, that people hardly expect any thing better; yet they are obliged to observe the appointed hour, or they might possibly forego the profit of the occasion. Thus sometimes the precious hours of thousands are irretrievably lost through the neglect of a few tardy officials. Let these thousands of lost hours be aggregated into one amount, and their worth to industry estimated, and the waste would appear enormous.

PUNCTUALITY AS TO PROMISES.

There are other cases in which the pinch of punctuality is not sufficiently felt, and disappointment and inconvenience may annoy, and possibly much pecuniary loss be incurred. For instance, how often mechanics and other producers engage to furnish articles by a certain date, and then fail of accomplishment! In fact, through all the circles of business, promises as to time are frequently broken: hence losses of money, or comfort at any rate, of good feeling, and perhaps of amicable relations. This is a matter of ordinary experience. The fact is, that many a man, in promising the completion of work at a certain day, has but a vague idea of the time necessary for the performance. He goes by guess. His judgment as to time and movement has not been cultivated. Perhaps he is constitutionally defective, and can measure days and hours scarcely much better than the senseless clock with its machinery askew.

DISASTROUS, LACK OF PROMPTITUDE.

In human affairs, there are crosses and losses innumerable and incalculable through lack of promptitude. At the first battle of Bull Run, the long delay of one division in the morning's march was an incidental cause of that lamentable defeat. Had our army got into action as early as was intended in the commander's plan, a decisive victory would have probably been won several hours before those re-enforcements arrived which turned the scale in favor of the enemy. It was probably a miscalculation as to time on somebody's part which prevented the pontoon-bridges from reaching Fredericksburg coincidently with the army, and thus delaying Burnside's great movement and leading to ultimate defeat. History records numerous instances of similar disasters.

EARLY ATTENTION TO THE TIME-FACULTY.

Now, as this defect as to time is often a constitutional infirmity, it should be understood at the very outset of education, and be remedied by the most assiduous culture. It may be discovered, by a little attention; what the native capacity of children is in this respect. See whether they are prompt at school, church, or any other place, at the appointed moment. Note whether they seem to lose all idea of time in play or talk when some pressing duty is before them. Should there appear an unconsciousness of duration, then they must be watched, and trained accordingly. As a disciplinary exercise, let them be put in many ways to the exact observation of time in the course of ordinary duty. In some affairs, certain operations require a certain measurable period of time for their accomplishment. The usual routine of every day in household or farm matters is divided into several parts appertaining to one thing and another. In the course of experience and habit, calculations are very readily made in respect to the quantity of time demanded by each, so that every thing may be attended to and finished in order. But the young generally need some special discipline before they can accurately adjust one thing to another in their engagements. Some require very much care for thé purpose. If they should be neglected in this matter by the first parental educators, they would be likely to go through the whole subsequent life, confused themselves, and confusing others. Innumerable people continue all their days in this unfortunate predicament, and just from the lack of foresight and discipline.

HELP FROM THE TIMEPIECE.

Accustom, therefore, children to notice particularly the hours, the half-hours, and even the minutes, occupied in any regular work or duty. Let it be, however, insisted on that performance shall be thorough and without fluttering haste. In this way, they will learn how to portion out time to its several uses. They will be educated into a substantial and reliable judgment as to the seasons of regular duty.

There are occasional transactions which also may well be made lessons. In doing errands at a store or a neighbor's or anywhere else, let the time of going and coming at ordinary speed be carefully noted. As children are fond of special exercises if they but be made agreeable, let them guess how long it will take to walk or run a certain distance and back again, or to make a certain number of motions with the feet or hands in imitation of work, as in the Kinder-garten plays. Suppose any new work is to be undertaken: let there be guesses as to the time occupied. Indeed, no matter what the operation is, it will serve to discipline the young to mark time with precision, and to form habits of adjusting movements to movements with an economical accuracy, which shall be a lifelong benefit to themselves and everybody who has to do with them.

MEASURING TIME BY THE SUN.

It is a good plan, furthermore, to have children measure time by the place and the progress of the sun. Let them guess the time of day by the sun's position in the sky, and then refer to the timepiece to see how near the precise moment they have hit. Let such an exercise be pursued till the hour of day, at any place of the sun, may be quite accurately determined. A similar course might be pursued in respect to the moon and the stars, for the sake of a more thorough education of the faculty, and perhaps for occasional and valuable use in emergencies that might arise. Indeed, the first idea of time came from the regular movements of the heavenly bodies. Hence originated those divisions of duration which are named in the languages, and govern the doings of all the world. These phenomena of the heavens perpetually teach and remind mankind of the importance of method or economy in the use of time. No lesson pertaining to life's practical affairs is inculcated on a grander scale than this. It is written on the expanse of the firmament. It is illustrated by revolving globes. Parents! shall this wisdom, so mightily and momentously vouchsafed, be lost to your children because you fail to interpret it to their understandings and impress it on their hearts?

ORDER.

In the works of God there is a certain order, or methodical arrangement, which is best adapted to the end for which they were made. Not only organic forms of matter, but the operations by which they accomplish their uses, exhibit this perfect adaptation of one thing to another, and of means to ends. Thus they give an all-important lesson to man for his own works and ways. In human affairs, it is by a similar systematization that the greatest good is brought to pass.

A SPECIAL FACULTY.

It is supposed that there is a special mental faculty which takes cognizance of order. It gives to the individual the ability to notice and appreciate it in things around; and also the ability to do things, and keep things himself, according to the same rule. There are sometimes wide differences between one person and another as to the native strength of this faculty. To be convinced of this, we have but to recall our experiences with various people. One has a place for every thing, and keeps every thing in its own place. Such a one is thoroughly systematic in business. That thing is done first which in good judgment should come first. He knows when his work is completed. There are no hurried runnings or flurried huddlings to finish up what was supposed to be already finished. With him, "done" means *done*, and is truly so. His anticipated leisure is not all cut up or cut short in the least by his own neglects. As far as depends on himself, he is always sure of time for pastime. Just like the sun that regularly shines on him, he knows his exact path, and his exact place in that path, at every hour from morning until evening; and then he knows when his day is done, as the sun knows his going-down.

How entirely different from this is the constitutional character and prevalent habits of another person! Indeed, how many there are, who, as to a systematic disposition of things, are about as much to be calculated on as the dust blown and tossed by the wind! They cannot calculate on themselves. They are disturbed by tendencies which have crept into their natures from some progenitor: so these tendencies impel them to and fro, up and down, evermore, because no educating hand came in good season to the rescue.

Such being the contingencies of poor human nature, they should be looked after without fail, and right early. The educator should understand the child's native mark of ability to appreciate order and conform to its laws. It can soon be seen whether much attention shall be required. Be the faculty stronger or weaker, it should be put to its use, and consequently under discipline, the same as the other intellectual powers. The parent's loving heart will be glad at an easy task; and the same heart, together with a quickening conscience, will prompt to perseverance and insure success in the more difficult case.

HOW TO DISCIPLINE THE FACULTY.

Let us now consider what a child may be put upon quite early in the way of training the faculty of order.

I once knew a child, not more than nine months old, who was disturbed and uncomfortable when some prominent article in the room, as a table, work-stand, or chair, was not in its accustomed place. He would point with his finger, together with a significant, indeed an imploring expression of his eye, to the thing in its irregular position. This child, no doubt, possessed the faculty of order in very strong constitutional development. But we may infer from the instance, that children, on the average, may, in this respect, be quite early trained to strength and accuracy. A child who only creeps might be set to the use of pushing a displaced chair into its position in line with the other chairs. When he shall get fairly upon his feet, he might have a care, according to strength, that any article of furniture in the room, when out of place, should be put right. Such a charge would be not only a discipline in the plan of the parent, but it would be an actual pleasure in the idea of a child. He wants to move; he cannot bear to be still: if he can do things to a certain end like others, and especially if he can gratify others by his activities, he is in his life's delight.

CARE OF PLAYTHINGS AND CLOTHES.

Accustom a child to take the best possible care of his own playthings,— to have a special place for them when not in use. They should never be thrust confusedly down, and lie in a jumble, as so often happens, but be laid by with as much regard for convenient arrangement and neatness as any implement of adult industry may be put away, each where it belongs. This order about playthings will be an important preparation for order in the work-things of after-life.

Still further: let children be educated to keep their own clothes in the best possible disposure in the drawer, chest, or closet, or wherever they may be placed. Let each article, however small, have its own particular position, where, if need be, it might be found in the dark.

Their clothes, on being taken off for the night, should be put in a certain definite and appropriate place: not here at one time, and there at another, but in the best position for airing; and each article in such a manner as to be most easily come at, even without light. Thus, in the case of fire and the necessity of quick escape, whether at home or abroad, whether at the house of a friend or at a strange hotel, the clothes could at least be snatched by the hand, if there should not be time to put them on. By an orderly habit of this sort, thousands in the conflagrations of the past would not have been driven almost naked from the burning into opposite elements, which diseased them perhaps for life by their inclemencies.

HOUSEHOLD MATTERS.

When children shall be old enough to assist in household affairs or other duties, it is of much consequence that they should do every thing according to that exact succession of operations by which any kind of work can be most speedily and most thoroughly accomplished. Days and weeks, and, in a long life, even months, are lost to some, because the precise firstly, secondly, thirdly, &c., are not linked into habit. The buzzing, clattering, rumbling factories of all sorts might instruct such wasters; for here must be a certain beginning, a regular progress, and a definite and sure completion.

Early and fixed habits of this sort will have great influence on their own industrial conditions and success in the far future. In the case of girls, the practice of order cannot be too early commenced, and it should never be intermitted. They grow up right in the midst of those matters and things, the like of which is to make their own chief duty as wives and mothers. Laxity of order in girlhood, unreformed then, will run very probably a disturbing force through all their housekeeping future.

BOYS.

In the case of boys, they may be put to apprenticeships in which there is a necessity for a certain order, as in mechanical trades and the use of machinery. They may be compelled to be systematic in their vocations to a certain extent; yet, in other affairs, they may fall into exceeding laxity and confusion. Whatever, therefore, they have to do, within or around the house, should be performed with regularity and precision; not only because it is best for the occasion, but because it will be a valuable discipline toward their future.

NEATNESS.

Personal neatness comes under this head of order. This, with some constitutions, will be found to require much training and discipline. There are children, who, from a native instinct, have a strong abhorrence of any soiling of their persons or clothes. They are early quite sensible of any lack of neatness about a room. Others are much the reverse. These seem to enjoy dirt and disorder as much as others do the best condition of things. These disorderly natures must be early looked to, and continually watched as they go along up, that, through mere discipline, they may have that habit of neatness which will be necessary for the comfort and satisfaction of others, if not for their own. Many a man, slovenly in his person and in his business, many an untidy woman and housekeeper, might have been blessed with at least average habits of neatness, had they been properly disciplined in their early homes. Such children should be set particularly to put and keep things in order about a house or the surroundings. If any thing should be out of place, they, above all others, should be set to put it in place. If they must go, in case of need, up into the garret, down into the cellar, to some distant out-house, or away into a field, so much the better. The farther they shall have to run, the more impressive and profitable the practical lesson. This sort of task should be made an imperative duty, to be continued as long as is necessary. By this discipline, such faulty organizations will be forced into the desirable habits, even against their own natures.

There is a neatness in work, and in the way of doing a thousand little things, which many people, for the lack of early education, do not possess. They will drop and slop, spill and spatter, in every direction, simply because they are not trained to steadiness of hand, carefulness of the foot, or quick observation of the eye. Pains and perseverance with such children will save much trouble under the parental roof, and will prevent them, doubtless, from innumerable discomforts and a thousand chagrins in their own future home. But let it be most especially remembered, that example will be unspeakably more powerful than precept. The young will hardly practise order amid the surrounding confusion of their elders. The disorder in which they have been brought up, and to which they have been from the earliest accustomed, is quite likely to be the earliest and habitual experience of their own rising families, and to become, possibly, the unprofitable inheritance of generations still beyond.

AN APPEAL.

Parents! for your own sakes in the dear home, for the sake of loved children in their future abodes and vocations, and for the sake of that common usefulness every one owes to his kind; for the sake of some higher and wider good your son or daughter may be providentially called to accomplish, — do not omit a duty comparatively so easy as the one now enjoined.

Train your young families to that methodical arrangement, to that best order, so necessary to give to art and industry and to all virtuous endeavors the highest success. By such a habit, work which *must* be done, however coarse, may be done in a way which is not only the shortest and the easiest, but which may have even something like a gracefulness about it. By this, the humblest task may have an adornment.

The inferior animals, each after its kind, are orderly by instinct, and might instruct the intelligences put over them in dominion. Inanimate nature, close by and all around, teaches those who labor in its midst the same lesson. How instructive are soil, water, air, heat, and light, as they work and build up blooming and fruitful vegetation! The same wisdom comes from the far silent heavens: with a power mightier than any human speech, they proclaim the *necessity* of system. They show forth the beauty, the majesty, the divine perfectness, of order, while they declare the glory of God.

CONCLUSION.

Other specific topics belong to the subject of these suggestions, and might properly have been considered. But this division of the volume has been extended much beyond the original design. It is hoped that the patience of readers will hold out for some closing thoughts, which may still further elucidate and confirm the theory presented.

It is a well-known fact, that the majority of mankind do not begin to study specifically and minutely the substances on which they are to operate through all their industrial lives, until they get into apprenticeship or into actual business. Then there must be disadvantage and loss, for a time, in proportion to the ignorance. In some cases, this ignorance continues quite palpably and injuriously through all their vocational course. Now, the training which has been indicated is a process of fitting one, in a degree, for all sorts of business whatever; a process begun with the very opening of the eyes and the putting-forth of the hand. Indeed, Nature is continually striving to educate the perceptive faculties; and would really double and quadruple their development and attainments, if we would let her have her own methods, and lend her a helping hand amid the multitude of objects which might confuse the young learner's attention.

There are certain individuals whose peculiar organization will make them sharp-sighted; will place things, and all their qualities, before them just as they are, notwithstanding the distracting circumstances of number, variety, and even disorder: but these are comparatively few. The majority need help and showing, that the most may be made of the materials around. This must be evident from the exercises in objects and qualities which have been here proposed; for how few, without advice, would pursue these matters in the best way, and to the most profitable extent! Indeed, how has the whole world gone blunderingly along with the idea, that education consists in words, — words wide apart from the things to which they belong! It has scarcely occurred to educators generally, that, in presenting things to the learner, they must almost necessarily present words — nouns, adjectives, and verbs — which would stick to these things like their color in the day-time, or as their temperature does both day and night.

HOW A GOOD JUDGMENT COMES.

There is a common saying about certain individuals something like this: "He has an excellent judgment; he is remarkable for his judgment." Now, what is meant? It is this: He knows what things are in their qualities and relations, and he knows what to do with them to the best possible advantage. Innumerable instances in the various avocations of life might be adduced in illustration. How common it is for a citizen to be called on to appraise the goods of a neighboring estate, or, as a public officer, to make valuations of property for taxes! In such cases, a practical knowledge of commodities is all-important. We may take the most striking and instructive instances from these very times. Millions of money are lost to the nation through the ignorance of commissaries, quartermasters, contractors, and other providers for our armies, through the lack of that early and continued education of the observing faculties which has now been advised. If the loss, for the most part, comes from any other cause, it must be from a criminal dishonesty, deserving the punishment of a penitentiary from a cheated country.

VIVID RECOLLECTIONS IMPORTANT.

Furthermore, a great deal of business is done in the way of trade, without the actual presence and inspection of the commodity to be bought and sold. In this case, much is to be trusted to the honesty or honor of the seller. Nevertheless, a great deal depends, on both sides, upon the actual knowledge of things previously acquired. Without such knowledge, the buyer must take the seller's word; and, without this knowledge, the seller himself may unintentionally mislead: for in both of their memories and conceptions there may lie a confused mass of things, designated by certain names. As for the absolute qualities, fitnesses, and values, it may be the merest guess-work with both. Or, if but one of the parties is ignorant, he must go by guess, or trust implicitly to the integrity of the other. Now, let a thorough acquaintance with objects and their qualities be obtained, and there they lie in the memory in all distinctness. There is no confusion. The mind's eye sees similar commodities in the distant ship or warehouse, or anywhere else, about as clearly as the physical eye would see them lying beneath the face. The memory, as a general rule, performs its office well or ill, just in proportion as the original perceptions are disciplined and developed; so that, in a large portion of business transactions, what is good judgment depends on distinct and accurate recollections.

DISTINGUISHED MEN.

The histories of many distinguished persons show, that it was a culture quite independent of prescribed educational forms which made them useful and eminent. Among the extraordinary men of our own country are those whose literary advantages were exceedingly limited. They simply exercised their naked faculties on whatever came before them, or lay in any providential line of duty. They might have had some one power, like individuality or eventuality, in uncommon strength. This, spontaneously, leading the way, might have brought concomitant powers into action and increasing ability. All the faculties were employed upon the objects, the events, the realities of the present world, and state of things; while their privileged contemporaries were engaged on abstract books and chapters, sentences and words. Although these students of real life might be quite inaccurate in the nice uses of language, yet they obtained the weightier matters of a useful education. Such men, nevertheless, generally possess an adequate ability at expression, as far as it is necessary simply to convey their own ideas. Indeed, these observers and doers often have a remarkable facility of speech. This comes from the very nature of their education. They somehow pick up words appropriate to all the things, qualities, relations, actions, and transactions within their notice; and those words are presented naturally and easily with the subjects to which they belong. If there should be any defect at all, it is that of some little point which they might have rectified themselves, as many do, by a strenuous and determined self-discipline. The strongest men in our nation, the centres of momentous circles of affairs, may be excelled by school-girls of fifteen as to verbal and grammatical niceties. The ability adequate to the Presidency of the nation or to a Cabinet secretaryship does not depend on verbalities obtained at school or college, but on an acquaintance with things and actions and principles; a knowledge of individual, social, municipal, civil, military, national, and international realities. Washington's success, at the head of armies and administrations, was the result of that sound judgment which had been matured amid present substances, passing events, and pressing emergencies.

BOOKS, NEVERTHELESS.

Let it not be supposed, by what precedes, that an unwarrantable discarding of books is advised. It is simply meant that books shall not come into use so early, so numerously, and so unintermittedly, as to stifle and dwarf the faculties instead of aiding to strengthen them. The distinguished men alluded to improved themselves by reading as they had opportunity; and, in one respect, they read with a peculiar advantage. Their preliminary experience with the world's naked realities enabled them to take hold of language with a strong, effective grasp, as if words were palpable handles to the meanings underneath. They labored, however, under many and great disadvantages. Their improvement came without system, — now and then, — here a little, and there a little.

With our present command of means, we ourselves should seek for our children that education which begins exactly in the right place and at the right time, and which proceeds in the best order, and in those directions, and to that extent, which shall make the largest and fullest measure of good.

Dear fellow-educators!—with what gentle touches of nature's elements, as with his own tender fingers, does the infinite Parent awaken his immortal offspring to consciousness and thought! Why shall we not follow these divine intimations? Be assured that they run, with unbroken continuance, into grand rules of development and great infallible signs along the way of everlasting progress.

Leaving much that might well be said, were there space, we will now consider the unfolding of those affections, without which the intellect, however mighty amid material things, is yet but weak and poor, and can never rise to those realms where angels teach, and none but the loving grow wise.

A LETTER FROM THE AGENT OF THE MASSACHUSETTS BOARD OF EDUCATION.

[After the preceding suggestions were first sent to the press, circumstances occasioned a considerable delay in the printing. In the mean time, the discipline in view has been fast gaining in public favor. I submitted the "Suggestions," as soon as I could, in sheets, to the large-minded and efficient State official above mentioned; and I am fortunate in the permission to place his letter here as a most seasonable and sufficient indorsement of my own views on the subject.]

Boston, April 28, 1863.

Rev. Warren Burton.

My dear Sir, — I am very glad to learn that you are about to publish a work for parents, embodying the results of your varied experience, wide observation, and long study. The portion of this volume which I have had the pleasure of reading abounds in wise and practical suggestions of great importance. Your hints on "Object-teaching" will accomplish much good, if they lead parents to the early and proper discipline of the observing faculties of their children. So far as relates to intellectual training, I heartily concur in the sentiment of Ruskin, "The more I think of it, I find this conclusion more impressed upon me, that the greatest thing a human soul ever does in this world is *to see* something, and tell what it saw in a plain way. Hundreds of people can talk, to one who thinks; but thousands can think, to *one who can see*."

The importance and methods of "Object-teaching" have been a frequent topic of my lectures at teachers' institutes and normal schools for more than six years. The system is gradually working its way into our schools, and, when in skilful hands, with the happiest results. I have spent several weeks during the last year in visiting the best "object-schools" in the country, especially in New York, Albany, New Britain, Conn., Toronto, C.W., and Oswego, N.Y. This system has been more fully and successfully applied in the schools of the latter place than anywhere else in this country. As a result, the primary schools of Oswego, which a few years since were in a low condition, have been raised to a degree of excellence, probably not surpassed, if equalled, in this country. I visited all the schools of the city, with a single exception, in order to observe the working of the system under a great variety of circumstances, and with all classes of children, the rich and the poor, Germans, French, Irish, and Scotch, as well as Americans. So celebrated have these schools become, that Oswego is now a sort of Mecca for educators from nearly all the loyal States. During a visit of less than two weeks in that city, I observed representatives present from several distant States, including teachers, committees, and superintendents. This, I was told, was but the usual number of visitors from abroad. While I should dissent from some views and methods there adopted, the system, as a whole, is, in my judgment, practical, philosophical, and admirably adapted to young children.

But this drill ought to begin long before the school

age. *The parent* should daily give training-lessons in common things. I value this book as one designed and fitted to make parents "object-teachers;" to convince them that the facts and objects surrounding the child in every-day life should be the earliest and most effective instruments in developing his powers; and that thus habits of close, accurate, and exhaustive observation should be early formed.

BIRDSEY G. NORTHROP,
Agent Mass. Board of Education.

TOPICS

OF

RELIGIOUS EDUCATION.

NOTE.

LET it not be understood that the writer thinks this division of his volume at all complete. He is aware, that, on the topics here considered, more might be said, and certainly a great deal better said, than will now be found. There are some kindred points which he has not touched upon at all, or but very briefly. He has followed the course of thought and sentiment which providentially ran through his own mind. On some other occasion, perhaps, subjects here neglected, or treated but slightly, will receive from him more worthy attention. At any rate, if readers will consult other writers on education, as they are sincerely besought to do, they will find some of the deficiencies of this humble work quite amply supplied.

THE FIRST KNOWLEDGE OF THE CREATOR.

WHAT is the best method of communicating the first ideas and knowledge of the Divine Being to a child?

It requires forethought and wisdom to make this communication in a manner worthy of the most high, most holy, and most loving Object of thought. We know how deep are earliest impressions; how strong and uneradicable are the ties of association: how unspeakably important, then, are the associations which should surround the first idea of the greatest and best of all beings in the mind of a child! He is to be reverenced and loved more than all others; and there should be nothing which could possibly detract from the most full and perfect enjoyment of this chief, central, supreme Image in the mind. Every thing should be in harmony with all the perfect attributes of God, as these shall be rationally and truly understood in maturer life. The associations of the first communication, at a time when these attributes can hardly be apprehended, will go along with the opening understanding and affections, and be connected with even the best idea of the Divine that may come in to the unfolding capacities. It seems, therefore, that the first knowledge of the Creator should be communicated on some chosen occasion, and by the person who, from relationship and loving care, will best represent the divine attributes. This person is the parent.

The first consideration respects that one particular name of the several belonging to the Infinite One, by which he shall be first designated to a child. Were the title, Our Father in heaven, or Our heavenly Father, the first to be impressed upon the infant memory, it would not, at this early age, be associated with the deep overflowing love and all the watchful care of the parental relation. These qualities would not come into view, except with growing experience. It seems to me, therefore, that the name GOD should be the first through which the mind should have this earliest knowledge. This is the first and the oftenest used in the Bible. Indeed, in point of time, the Divine Being was God, before he was a Father to the child. The relation of Father does not exist till the offspring has existence; but from eternity he is the self-existent God. This name, therefore, should be the first presented, as indicating a Being whom he cannot see, but who is the Maker of all he does see. It would be a new name to him. It should be presented so as to be a most impressive name; moreover, one, above all, most pleasant in remembrance.

The Divine Being is generally first made known in connection with some one of his works. "Who made it?" is one of the earliest questionings of a child, as if he had an intuitive notion that every thing must have a maker. "God made it," is an answer and a belief written among the earliest memories of all the Christian generations. Now, what object shall be the first occasion of using the holy Name, and of expressing the fact of divine creation? It seems to me, it should be the most beautiful, majestic, glorious representative of God presented by the whole material creation, — the sun. Nothing so attracts the infant's eye as the light; for the light belongs to the eye, and the eye belongs to the light. The very flame from the fireside and the candle attracts his gaze before he has looked beyond the walls of the nursery; and, at first, more than any thing else within them. How, then, must the brightness of the sun fasten his inexperienced attention! But not that of the noonday luminary. These splendors dazzle away the eye, and prevent calm, impressive contemplation. It is the sun, then, in its milder glories, not overpowering the vision to blindness, but filling it with pleasure and admiration, through which the idea of God should be first conveyed. It is through the rising light that the idea of the Father of lights should first ascend into the soul's firmament, and thence illumine all ideas and all knowledge beneath.

With some special care, almost any child might be led to gaze at and admire the morning twilight and the mounting sun. If there is any thing in all nature which can fasten his vision in the intensest observation, it is this. He may be pleased with the tree-blossom, or the flower from the garden or field, or any other bright object; he may be amused, may be delighted, with these beautiful little things: but it is not with such that I would first associate the name of the great and glorious God. The first and deepest impression of the Almighty Creator should not be with what is little and pretty; which can be held in the hand, played with, and picked to pieces by the fingers, and destroyed. No; but carry him, as early as he shall be able to individualize the object, able to separate it from the horizon of earth and sky, from contiguous cloud or hill, to behold the rising sun. A child is attracted not only by form and color, but by motion. Here he beholds the most perfect form amid the most charming hues, — a glory too mild to dazzle and pain the eye; and this, in grand magnificent movement, a double enchantment to the fastened gaze. Let this spectacle become a frequent and a most desirable pastime to the opening, the admiring, the wondering little soul. Then, when there shall be sufficient maturity, choose the most fitting opportunity — one when all the circumstances shall be most agreeable and appropriate — to pronounce the adorable Name, together with one of the greatest facts in creation, as a remembrance. "God made the sun." Let the child pronounce these words after you: "God made the sun." He does not know yet who God is. This knowledge will come in due time. But the supreme Name is henceforth and for ever associated with the most glorious material creation. God made the sun. The first eternal truth is written upon an imperishable memory. Here begins that instruction in religion, in love, in devotion to God, which is to consecrate and shed blessed influence upon all other instruction. This is the first opening of the soul's temple for the Divinity to be there enthroned for worship. Henceforth the name God, caught by the infantile ear, will make impression, and especially if heard in worship. The child hitherto, in the family devotions, may have been quiet, and as if seemingly listening; but the language of the service most probably slipped over his ear, dropping nothing into his soul. The holy names and titles were to him, perhaps, no more than the most insignificant particles of speech. But now the name of Him who made the great round, bright, beautiful sun, coming up in the east, surrounded by charming colors, —*that* name will mean something, will be thought of, will be remembered, *felt*. How reverently, then, should it be spoken in the hearing of the child! It may be well for him to observe that it is pronounced with some nice peculiarity of tone, separating it markedly from other words. It should not be a tone to touch his spirit with any thing like fear, any thing disagreeable, or any thing ever afterward to be remembered as out of taste, or not accordant with all gentle or grand harmonies. Let there be no nasal twang, no rough or peculiarly odd pronunciation; let there be nothing which shall not afterwards mingle sweetly with the very best melodies of memory. Sometimes the speaking of a word, with the slightest lowering and softening of the voice, is impressive; far more emphatic, indeed, than force or loudness. There may be again the least perceptible pause before utterance, so that the holy Name shall stand out distinctly from its connections more than the other words, and yet not to such a degree as to cause any discordant and inappropriate hiatus. Certain persons are able to express humility, reverence, and love, all combined, as they take the divine Name upon their lips. This cannot be expected of all, any more than that all should sing in perfection; but all who love their children, and feel that they have the most sacred of all human duties to perform toward them, can strive for the best preparation, and can approximate perfection in proportion to natural gifts and earnest endeavors.

There will come in connection those adjunctive words, signifying the qualities and attributes of the Divine; such as the Almighty, the Most High, the Eternal, the Most Holy, Gracious, Blessed, together with others. A child cannot at first receive the full meaning of these, any more than he can take in the full idea of God. It is not at all necessary that he should. As his mind opens, they will assume larger and larger breadth in it, and deeper and deeper meaning, taking hold of the affections. All these epithets should be so used as to inspire the sincerest, the very best devotion of the soul, the fullest reverence and love. Almighty and most merciful God!—this phrase from the Christian ages often makes the commencement of prayer. Infinite power, with infinite tenderness, is attributed to that one Being who alone can hear and answer prayer to the uttermost. How should such an expression be consecrated in the memory and and the heart of a child? The same may be said of other sacred phrases.

There are the human appellations of the Deity, more home-coming and heart-touching because drawn from the analogies of the home and the heart,— Our Father in heaven, or Our heavenly Father. Some, perhaps, may prefer first to present the idea of the Creator under one of these phrases. They give to the child at once the idea of love, gentleness, care, and protection, as far as the parental title already stands for these qualities in his apprehension. But, after all, this Being is unseen, and can scarcely be comprehended thus early by these tender analogies. He is yet a mystery; and I should prefer to have him presented first by a new and mysterious name, God. The term "father" can be applied to many all around, — to the vile, to the worst of human beings: that of God belongs to the One. That name can never belong to any other. Then let that one Name be a central name in the firmament of the understanding; the greatest, highest, holiest, best; even as that Being must be whom it images forth. But the tenderer name of Father, in due time, can be easily associated with the Divine. In conversations about the loving and beautiful character of God, he can be likened to a Father in faithful care and tenderness. There can be easily impressed upon the child all that is most lovable, and best suited to bring out toward the heavenly Parent his tenderest affections. His earliest prayer will be that which belongs both to infancy and age, and all the life between,—the all-comprehending one taught by the Lord. Though the word "God" is not expressed within its compass, yet the child will readily associate our Father with that mysterious name which is first and greatest in remembrance.

Besides the most majestic and appropriate illustration of creative power and glory, various other objects in nature should be made the mediums of religious instruction. Perhaps the new moon, as it appears after an interval, and which is not, like the older moon, a repeated nightly spectacle, might to the infant mind be one of the best tokens of the Divine Power. The child may hardly remember to have seen it the month before. There it is, the delicate crescent, a bright silvery bow upon the edge of the golden, mellow twilight. It is as if it had just been created, and placed there by an invisible hand. How it attracts and fastens the little wonderer's gaze! Let it be said in due time, after the first great impression from the monarch luminary, " God made the new moon."

There, too, is the beaming, melting, richly flowing evening star: let its brightness, its beauty, its charmingness, fall into the tender memory with the name of God. That is a most touching instance of a child's startled apprehension of creative power expressed in a sweet little poem : —

> " Presently, in the edge of the last tint
> Of sunset, where the blue was melted in
> To the faint golden mellowness, a star
> Stood suddenly. A laugh of wild delight
> Burst from her lips; and, putting up her hands,
> Her simple thought broke out expressively,
> ' Father, dear father, God has made a star!' " *

---

* See " Sacred Poems," by N. P. Willis.

The whole starry host of the heavens, at a rightly chosen occasion, should be made to uplift, to solemnize, to fill the little mind with the power, majesty, and glory of God.

But the earth is written all over with lessons on the goodness and greatness of the Creator. There are the flowers, with their beauty and fragrance, whereby to express the blessed name and character of God. There are the birds, all life, motion, and music, through whom his name and his praise may, as it were, be sung to the delighted ear. Showers and rainbows; the forth-putting verdure and foliage on field and forest in the spring, as if an invisible worker every day did more and more for the watching eye to admire, — these also may lift the thought toward God. Little purling brooks, and great sweeping rivers; the soft, green hills, and the blue and grand mountains; the dark storm-cloud, the swift lightning, and the thunder's marvellous voice, — should all be made to tell of God. But, if these mightiest exhibitions of nature should speak in majesty, they should also be made to utter forth the divine benignity and love.

Few children are permitted to look with their early eyes upon the great and grandly impressive ocean. Let such as are vouchsafed the spectacle associate it with Him who holds its unsounded depths and sublime boundlessness in the hollow of his hand.

The human being is, in his first consciousness, surrounded by the divine works. They are the first observed; they give the earliest impressions. They should all of them be made to declare the existence and character of God. But language is to be used, and this by the Parent through which these works are to address and instruct the soul. As early as possible, and as much as possible, this language should be that of God's holy word. There are passages which beautifully or grandly set forth the divine attributes. The child has already, with his earliest utterances, consecrated his innocent lips and his opening soul with the prayer of the Lord Jesus. Let him also commit to memory other precious portions of Scripture. Before he shall have learned to read, let the instruction, parents, be distilled as heavenly dew from your own lips. How it will fall upon his soul, and make it mellow and fruitful, even as the paths of God drop fatness!

The Old Testament, and especially the Psalms and the Prophets, abound in allusions to God's works and ways, and to his grand, his benignant, his charming attributes. But it is in the New Testament that are found the most inviting attractions toward God. There is the dear, first-learned prayer. There the Eternal and the Almighty is more particularly presented as a tender Father; and by whom? By Jesus, the Son,— the blessed, the beloved, the most gentle and compassionate, the most winning being ever seen on earth in human form. Now, why shall not the child commit to memory numerous passages from all these sacred inspirations? With your tender invitations, with your sweet encouragements, with your own song-like lips, how much might you lay upon his impressible memory before he can even read? This will shine out with more and more meaning as years increase, and will send gleam after gleam into his understanding, and fervor upon fervor into his heart. Heed not those, who, in this case, cry out against the uselessness and absurdity of words without knowledge. How many lessons do children study at home, overlooked by the parent, how many more at school, conveying scarcely an idea through the hard, unintelligible terms! and yet no objection is made, because *this* is supposed to be education. Is not religion also a matter of education? and must its length, breadth, depth, and height be the only science which the young intellect is required to see through at once, and thoroughly to measure from side to side and from foundation to summit? Let it not be asserted, that these instructions from the sacred oracles are peculiarly darkening or burdening to the young mind, when so very much else is imposed, which, in sad reality, is dry and hard and dark and burdensome. It will depend much on the manner of communication how it shall be received, and what effect it shall have; and, for this, your affection and wisdom are responsible. It belongs to you, more than to all the rest of the world, to make known, to the little ones waiting at your side, the glory of God as declared in the Book of books.

THE FIRST AND GREAT COMMANDMENT.

"Thou shalt love the Lord thy God with all thy heart, and with all thy soul, and with all thy mind, and with all thy strength."

WITH what cumulative and transcendent force of language is expressed the first and chief duty of man! The simple meaning doubtless is, that he must love the Creator more than any creature; he must love him supremely. To the Lord our God, to the Giver of all good, to the Father in the highest, belongs the strongest, the warmest, the most continually devoted love which is possible to human capacity.

Of all the commandments of the Most High, this is that one which should be most thoroughly impressed in the education of the young. The inculcation of it belongs to the heads of the family above all other teachers, as indeed does all religious nurture. But how can parents invite and train the child to love God supremely, when they do not themselves believe in the reality of the literal command, or in the possibility of fulfilment? Let us now see how the case apparently stands with many fathers and mothers of excellent repute, and who are regular attendants on Christian ministrations. If they should divulge their secret sentiments, would not the exclamation of each one be something like this?—"How is it possible to love a Being whom I cannot touch, cannot see, cannot hear; and who is infinitely, awfully great, to a degree unspeakably surpassing that with which I love my own nearest personal relatives, whom I can see and converse with, and who draw my heart to them by attentions, kindness, and an undoubted love, which they bestow on no other beings in the world? I can entertain a degree of gratitude toward the heavenly Parent; at certain times, I can feel even a warmer glow than this: but to *love* the universal and invisible Spirit above objects seemingly nearer and more personal to me; above friends, brothers, sisters, parents, children, and even wedded partner; in a word, to love him more than all these together, as seems to be implied,—oh! this is an utter impossibility. It must be that the language is extremely figurative, like much in the Scriptures; and, of course, is not to be literally fulfilled." Surely, judging from appearances, there prevails this utter unbelief in any positive ability fully to obey this great leading law of both the Mosaic and the Christian dispensations; or, if there is not a cold, careless unbelief, there is a palsying despair of the duty. There is at least an excessive indifference to it. In this condition of mind, parents cannot possibly train their children up to the Scripture requirement of love to God.

Now, if there could once be a clear understanding and belief of an ability to love the Divine Being above every other, would not the difficulty of doing so grow less and less, and at length entirely disappear? Would not parents realize, that the greatest possible favor they could confer on a beloved child would be the development of this affection, which is to become the essential life of the whole heart, soul, mind, and strength of the man?

It is proposed now to meet the case stated by showing that we have a capacity to love God to the degree expressed in the command; and that the language of Scripture, however strong and superlative, is no more than commensurate with the ability of fulfilment. We will first, however, dispose of a preliminary case. There is a very large number of people, taking them as they appear in the world around, who seem thus far to have experienced no degree of love or gratitude at all toward their Creator. It must be difficult for them to realize that they possess even the feeblest ability in this direction. They are yet to be convinced that they can love the Lord their God in the least. We will first meet their condition. In doing this, we shall be also better prepared to convince and persuade those who are partially experienced and are half-way believers.

A little analogical reasoning will conduct to the truth wanted. There are certain objects around us here, toward which we indulge affectionate feeling with different degrees of intensity and pleasure, according to our nearer or more remote relation. We love things inanimate, as country, home, and possessions therein. Next, we love friends, brothers, sisters, parents, children, wedded companion. The affection toward each one of these is different from that toward each other, conferring a pleasure of different kind and degree. The feeling toward inanimate objects is unlike that toward living beings. Friendship differs from the domestic loves; and these last are distinct one from another. There seems to be an independent mental faculty, through which each distinctive sentiment is exercised toward its appropriate object. Each is a separate fountain of happiness, set in the heart, and open to a perennial flow, if we choose to give it tending. But in all reason, in all consistency, must not another love be added to the list? Can it be, that the infinitely Beneficent should endow us with capacities to love and be happy in each other; indeed, to be attached even to things without life; and yet leave us destitute of a capacity by which to love HIM, the Author and Giver of all, the soul's own Father in the highest, the best of all beings, the loveliest of all, and consequently, of all beings, the most worthy of love? Oh, no! He whose highest attribute, whose innermost nature, is love, would certainly crown the series of loves by conferring the capacity to love himself, the primal source of love, in return. From the analogy of the human constitution, therefore, and leaving out of sight actual and individual experience, is there not the strongest probability that we are endowed with a distinct capacity appertaining to the Divine Being, whose function it is to entertain a special and a peculiar love toward him? Yes, we *can* love him, in some measure at least, because we were made to love him, as we love our earthly parents, being constituted so as to love them in return for their affection toward ourselves; or as, indeed, we love any relative with affection answering to affection. Must not the mere intellect, which acknowledges a perfect Creator, perceive by these analogies, that the human creature would hardly be complete without some sort of capacity to love him? With a consistent view of human nature, the man who could believe that he had no ability within him to love God, must also believe that something had been left out in his formation which ought to have been put in; or had been lost out of sight, and was worth being sought for until found.

We now come fairly to the all-important question in the present case : To what *degree* are we able to love God? *Can* we love him with all the heart and soul and mind and strength, according to the commandment? Can we train our children to this supreme affection? Have parents this supposed excuse of inherent inability in themselves and their offspring? Let us again try analogy. In the several distinct relations of life before mentioned, we naturally love the object of each in a degree proportionate to the nearness of that object in the series of relationships. In a well-trained family, the affection between brothers and sisters is stronger than that toward companions outside of the home. The affection of children toward parents is stronger than that toward each other. The love of parents toward children has a still stronger hold on the heart. The love between parents themselves, as husband and wife, if there be a true marriage, surpasses all other feelings and intimacies between fellow-creatures. Thus, as we go from the lower to the higher relations, and as the connection becomes more close and unbroken and indispensably necessary in the constitution of things, the more intense is the love. That person on earth who is the nearest in relationship, in place, and in intimacy, has the deepest and most thorough hold on our nature. Now, apply this rule of order, nearness, and intimacy, a step farther. The next higher Being, and the last, with whom we are in positive and certain relations, is the very Lord God. He is not the medium through which body and spirit come, but the very source from which they come. He is the Framer of the body, and the Father of the spirit. His own life and love, wisdom and power, are the essential origin of him who here appears in his image and likeness. There is no relative in the universe so near to man as the eternal

God. He is, in absolute truth, the everlasting Father. Beyond all others, therefore, he must necessarily be the highest, closest, best object of the heart. If, then, the heart shall be consistent with itself, true to its other relations, according to their degrees, it will permit this nearest, this first and eternal Relative to possess its love to the uttermost.

Still further: in the domestic relations, we ordinarily love, not only in proportion to the constitutional nearness of the relative, but also according to the opportunities for closeness, frequency, and continuance of communion. It is not necessary to run through these relations again. Suffice it to say, that the heavenly Father is not only actually nearer than any other being in the universe, but he never departs from this nearness if we would but recognize it. He is the ever-abiding centre and support of our nature. He is the life of our life, the inmost spirit of our spirit. Without his immediate and constant presence and power, we should fall to pieces as to body, and our souls even would be annihilated. We can go away from the nearest and dearest earthly friend,—the earth's width may be between us; but we cannot go away from God. Were all the other inhabitants of the world dead, and myself should survive, one and alone, God would be with me, the same as if my whole race were still existent. He would necessarily continue to be my inmost life, my own personal, infinitely loving, heavenly Father. I have, therefore, opportunities to commune with him, such as I have with no other being. At all times and in all places, he is with me, to be addressed, to be realized, as the source of all supply, the nearest and dearest of all friends. I have unceasingly open access to him; I have infinite opportunity. Why, then, should I not be able to love him with all that intensity of feeling expressed by the language of Holy Writ?

Does not all analogy conduct not only to the duty, but to the practicability of the duty, laid upon the faculties? If the divinely authoritative Word commands that we *must* love, an utterance from the secret depths of our own souls responds that we *can* love the Lord our God more than all beings beside.

But let us pursue our analogy one step farther still, and we shall arrive at a most important and crowning inference. Our best happiness is in those loving affections which we have been tracing, one above another, in our natures. Springing out of each kind of love, there is an enjoyment less or more in measure, according to the lower or higher character of the particular affection, and also according to its weakness or strength, or degree of development, in the individual soul. Now, we have seen that love toward God ought to be and can be the supreme affection; indeed, that no other affection can approach it in intensity and power. This being so, then high, strong, and absolutely supreme must be the *happiness* flowing forth from the full exercise thereof. From the inmost, the mightiest, the sovereign love must issue the highest felicity possible to a child of God, even a sovereign blessedness.

If the foregoing course of thought is conclusive, there must arise to any one seeking his best good, and especially to the parental heart bound up in dear offspring, this inquiry; viz., By what methods shall be developed this regal affection, through which the soul attains to its crowning bliss? If we have any adequate idea of the rich, the glorious object in view, we should be a contradiction to ourselves if we did not seek the means of attainment. Considering how we toil and struggle, and wrest both body and soul, for things which are as grains of sand to a kingdom's diadem, compared with the inheritance here presented, surely not to be awake to the worth of this priceless possession, and in most ardent, anxious inquiry how we shall secure it, would indicate that we are either idiotic or insane. Yes, here is human nature's utmost possible good, — the blissfulness which legitimately and necessarily flows from the inmost, the deepest, the largest, the most celestial, the most nearly divine capacity in our frame. The question now is, How shall we open this capacity, attain to a blissfulness which more than any thing else verifies to man below the lofty ejaculation, "In Thy presence is fulness of joy; at Thy right hand there are pleasures for evermore"?

As, all along, we have found an analogy between the particular religious affection in view and other affections, shall we not find a still farther analogy touching those means of development which we would now ascertain? Not only our affections, but all the various faculties of our nature, here reply and instruct.

Our powers generally become stronger and stronger in proportion to use. The body and limbs are made robust and sinewy by labor. The intellect is strengthened by exercise in study or in practical affairs. The elegant tastes are enhanced by cultivation. The conscience is quickened and sharpened by culture and use. The social affections grow by reciprocal and repeated attentions. The domestic loves deepen by ever-fresh interchanges of tenderness. We will illustrate, however, more at length by a sentiment, which, in this case, is particularly appropriate,—that of filial affection. In what manner is this excited, and made strong and delightful? Do not our own hearts and experience most clearly reply? It is by being constantly with parents, by receiving unremitted favors from their hands, by associating things given and acts done with the tenderness of a parent's love; it is by keeping the heart, as it were, open to the reception of that melting tenderness which flows in the tones, streams from the eyes, and distils from the whole countenance, of these earliest and best friends,—that filial love grows and is made strong. A good child is in the constant exercise of filial emotions; and, of course, there cannot but be a proportionate development and sweet satisfaction of the filial heart. But suppose, if possible, that a son, ever receiving favors from parents, should not often associate these favors with their tenderness; suppose that he should not care for their companionship; had as lief they would be absent as present: would this son love his parents in any degree commensurate with the affection and the favors unceasingly bestowed upon him? Certainly not. It is by frequent thinking about and feeling toward the parental benefactors that grateful love glows in the filial heart.

Finally, none of the faculties of our nature are felt, none are a source of enjoyment, till they are directed toward their appropriate objects, and exercised, and are thereby put into process of development. Now, let us apply these analogies to our relation to the heavenly Parent. Granting that we possess the strongest native capacity to love God, must it not remain in embryo, and be unfelt like the other affections, till it is directed to its proper object, and is exercised, is put to its intended use? Like them, how can it arrive at its fullest felicity without a conscious and close intimacy with that Being in relation to whom it was especially implanted? Our heavenly Father may bestow on us all we possess and enjoy; on his own part, he may love us and pity us to the utmost degree possible to his infinite nature: yet, if we think not of him, care not for him, hold no special communion with him, of course it will be impossible for us to love him, and enjoy the blessedness springing from this love. In this case, like all the others, there must be use before there can be development and strength, and the consequent delightful results.

We have, then, the all-important truth, that it is by *exercising* love toward God that it is strengthened into power, so as to become supreme over all the other affections of the soul. What, now, are some of the special methods of cultivating this holiest and happiest affection commanded in the divine Word, and confirmed by the very design and structure of man?

We seek the methods of that blessed work to be performed on ourselves and our families. We would love the Lord our God with all our heart, and with all our soul, and with all our mind, and with all our strength. What shall we do? First, this object of feeling being ever present in the uttermost nearness to our souls, we must cherish the consciousness of this fact of nearness until his presence shall be as familiar to our minds as the presence of parents is familiar to children in the native home. How much do reflective and tenderly affectioned children attribute to faithful parental care! It seems the very light and warmth and life of the house. In earliest years, they go to sleep at night, and leave this care yet near and watchful. They awake in the morning, and it is near and watchful still, as if no rest had been taken by it, or had been needed; and it is at work now, as it had been from their earliest remembrance, providing for their wants. They find themselves every new day encompassed by love and thoughtfulness as by the warmth and light. How tenderly they trust and love this unfailing presence! Now, just so should we train our children and discipline ourselves to regard the heavenly Parent's loving care. In the first place, he gives us to each other in the dear parental and filial ties. Indeed, he has distilled from his own bosom into our bosoms those sweet mutual affections with which they continually overflow. Next, he provides for the family wants, through the products of nature and the strength of the parental frame, in a manner without which we should all utterly perish. How much reason, then, have we to feel, to trust, to love, to rejoice in this presence, which pervades and fills the whole home; this Providence which never sleeps, although all other eyes are sealed; and which never shuts or draws back its hand!

Again: there are the divine works in nature; those through which sustenance and comfort come to the body, through which instruction comes to the understanding; those which display beauty, grandeur, and sublimity to the admiring sense. If the works and gifts of relatives and friends remind us of their kindness, and are ever exciting grateful affections anew, what should be the effect of works and gifts like these? The planets fail not to reflect the sun's golden beams, which they cannot help receiving; and why should not we be equally true to that "Father of lights," from whom cometh down every good and every perfect gift?

The devout Catholic makes his prayers one after another, according to the beads of his rosary, and believes himself drawn nearer and nearer to his God. To us and our children, creation is one boundless rosary, to lead on, and still ever to lead on, our hearts in the grateful fervors of devotion. Each individual object not only reminds of duty, but, by its special formation and use, should stir us to new emotions of adoring love. It is the rosary of the Church universal, and a gift from that common Father with whom is no respect of persons. It begins with the rocks and jewels of the mine, and is twined million-fold through the kingdoms of nature near; then it is wreathed in burning constellations above, and thence runs endlessly on before the eye of wondering and worshipping discovery; held fast and for ever by the hand of Him of whom it is written, "He telleth the number of the stars; he calleth them all by their names."

In another place, the scriptural presentations of the works of God are sufficiently commended to the heart and the memory. Here it may be useful to add, that the poetry of our native language is rich with allusions to the divine attributes as manifested in nature. Sacred verse especially abounds in such references as incitements to devotion. The training of the young to commit passages of this kind to memory would be among the best benefits bestowed by parental care. Early and peculiar associations, and an abiding influence with which many doubtless will sympathize, induce me to place here for illustration a well-known hymn of Watts. It is one of those which he entitled "Divine Songs, attempted in Easy Language for the Use of Children." Indeed, if it is "in easy language," and stoops to the simplicity of childhood, there is, notwithstanding, no fulness of strength, no greatness of mind, which might not be caught up by it, and borne away, as on cherubic wings, to contemplate the wonders of creation, and thus be inspired to sing the power, wisdom, and goodness of the Creator.

> "I sing the almighty power of God,
>   That made the mountains rise;
> That spread the flowing seas abroad,
>   And built the lofty skies.
>
> I sing the Wisdom that ordained
>   The sun to rule the day:
> The moon shines full at his command,
>   And all the stars obey.
>
> I sing the goodness of the Lord,
>   That filled the earth with food:
> He formed the creatures with his word,
>   And then pronounced them good.
>
> Lord, how thy wonders are displayed,
>   Where'er I turn mine eye;
> If I survey the ground I tread,
>   Or gaze upon the sky!
>
> There's not a plant or flower below
>   But makes thy glories known;
> And clouds arise, and tempests blow,
>   By order from thy throne.
>
> Creatures, as numerous as they be,
>   Are subject to thy care:
> There's not a place where we can flee,
>   But God is present there."

Besides these inspirations from what is sometimes called the "elder Scripture," there is another means of culture, which an illustration may possibly present more forcibly to notice. Suppose your earthly parent to pen a history of his life, embracing numerous acts of care and love for yourself, for brothers and sisters, during infancy, back beyond your own recollection; and also recording his various deeds of kindness, his admonitions, his hopes, his fears, his many, many trials, concerning his family during childhood and youth up to maturity. Suppose there to be an account, moreover, of his generous exertions for many others; of the part he had taken in great enterprises of philanthropy; of his endeavors in behalf of even the humblest and remotest race of men. Besides all these narrations of facts and circumstances, suppose there to be intermingled various precepts of surpassing wisdom and purity. Still farther: suppose there to be interspersed among the pages poetic effusions of transcendent beauty, pathos, and sublimity; effusions such as would take hold on the heart, and abide in the memory, filling you with the deepest sense of a genius consecrated to the highest and holiest aims. Now, if a memorial, such as has been imagined, should be left to be specially perused by your own eyes, and affectionately kept by your own hands, would you not prize it above every thing else which should come as property from the parental ownership? Would you not read it and read it over and over again, commit much of it to memory, get it by heart? Would a sentence or a line in that dear bequest escape your notice? Would you not feel that your father's spirit lived in every word? And in your repeated perusals of these writings, and meditations on their contents, as some new and precious meaning should open on your apprehension, would not your filial love kindle into renewed fervency, and perhaps into a livelier glow than ever before?

Our heavenly Father, through his appointed agents, has given such a record concerning himself. The parallel is, of course, not exact; but it is sufficiently so for our purpose. The Bible is filled with the revelations of his wisdom, with the instances of his beneficent affection toward his human offspring: its lyric and prophetic pages are radiant with emanations from that light which is inaccessible and full of glory. The whole varied volume, while it is righteous, august, awful, in authority and command, is also abounding in expressions of loving-kindness, tender mercy, unfailing compassion, and long-suffering toward erring children. We know the sacred contents: they need not be farther described. Now, should you dwell on the varied and wonderful writings, so lay up the rich treasures in your memory, so absorb their spirit into your heart (as you doubtless would in the previously imagined case), could it be otherwise than that your love toward God would grow proportionally intense, pervading and blessing your soul with a heavenly felicity? What amazing providences from the beginning, onward, all conducting to one grand result, — the deliverance of man from the slavery, degradation, and misery of sin! What heights, what depths, what vastness of wisdom and love, in the mission of the Saviour Son! And all this for you, your own particular self, and for each one of your children, as much as for any one that has lived. Oh! you and they could not hold in conception all this, could not realize it in heart, over and over, yea, continually, as might be done, without a love to the Lord God and Father of mercies, compared with which your present feeble feelings are as our spring's chilled and tardy vegetation compared with the summer's deep luxuriance of verdure and flowers.

Any opening of the soul to God in affection is a worship of itself. Every filial emotion toward the heavenly Parent, whether expressed or unuttered, and whenever it shall arise, is an approach toward him. It is a coming nearer and nearer to that conjunction of the finite spirit with the Infinite Spirit, in which alone there is perfect fruition. But there is a special and all-important influence to this end in definite and stated devotions. Let us now, then, more particularly consider that increase of loving piety which comes from the concentration of heart and soul and mind toward God in regularly recurring acts of worship.

It is a law of our nature, that, in relation to our friends, the more we express our sincerely kind feelings in language, and more especially in friendly acts, the more our affection deepens, the more fully does it possess the bosom. The effort of expression concentrates attention on the object, for some brief time at least, shutting out other things. Now, toward God we can perform no deed of charity; we can do nothing which is of the least benefit to him. With the exception of general obedience to his laws, we can outwardly manifest our hearts toward him only by acts and words of worship. But these acts and words are of the utmost importance to our spiritual life. In the same manner as expressions of kindness towards friends deepen that friendly love, as before mentioned, so does true worship quicken and deepen those feelings which spring from our relation to God. In the performance of this service, all other subjects being shut out from the mind, the religious faculties for the time are in earnest, unhindered action. They become stronger by the exercise, as any of the other faculties become stronger as they are put more and more to use. With this view, what encouragement to express our child-like love in frequent acts of devotion!

First, in private prayer. Let every rising day excite a lively gratitude to the unslumbering Guardian of the night, who has preserved us from harm during the senselessness and helplessness of sleep, and who is now the strength of the frame for another day's activity. Let a Christian poet's fire kindle the heart's earliest offering: —

> "To prayer, to prayer! for the morning breaks,
> And earth in her Maker's smile awakes:
> His light is on all, below and above, —
> The light of gladness and life and love.
> Oh! then, on the breath of this early air
> Send upward the incense of grateful prayer." *

Again: new and distinct instances of providential goodness may occur during the day. Why

---

* Henry Ware, jun.

should not each one elicit silent thanks, if not loudly ejaculated words? Should we not thank a fellow-mortal for inferior favors? We should certainly habituate our children to grateful expressions for occasional kindnesses of friends: why, then, should we not habituate them to a fresh renewal of devout gratitude to the all-gracious Friend for every new and distinct token of his goodness? "Seven times a day do I praise thee, because of thy righteous judgments," saith the Psalmist.

The season of rest again returning, let there be another act of devotion for the mercies of the closing day, and for the felt confidence that the same omnipotent care will preserve now in sleep as in nights before. Let the Christian poet before quoted aid into flame our evening sacrifice:—

> "To prayer! for the glorious sun is gone,
> And the gathering darkness of night comes on:
> Like a curtain, from God's kind hand it flows
> To shade the couch where his children repose.
> Then kneel while the watching stars are bright,
> And give your last thoughts to the Guardian of night."

There is one simple stanza which has come down from generation to generation in the religious training of the family. Millions of children doubtless have dropped into helpless unconsciousness as this passed out of the memory, yea, out of the heart over the lips. John Quincy Adams avowed in his old age, that this little verse, taught him in childhood by his tender, faithful mother, had been the prayer with which he had fallen to his nightly rest ever since. The chief ruler of a great nation could not dignify this prayer by the continued use of it in his age; but the use of it dignified him. He who humbled himself to be even as a little child was certainly exalted by so doing to be a shining central example to a whole nation of fathers, mothers, and children, through all coming time.*

Next, there is social worship; first and especially, that at the domestic altar. Friends, do you really desire for yourselves and your children to grow in a beatific love toward God? If so, then, as families, daily unite in a common thanksgiving for common favors, and particularly for family blessings. Let these clustered hearts thus statedly and feelingly express a pious gratitude that they are bound together in kindred ties, are a mutual good, and are enclosed in one dear, delightful home; and this service shall certainly

---

* "Now I lay me down to sleep," &c.

nurture that holiest love, which, as itself becomes supreme, shall more and more sanctify and enhance all the rest.

Lastly, there is the public worship of the sabbath. If the previous suggestions have been appreciated, it must be perceived that the services of the sanctuary are a farther and all-important means for the development of religious love. Here, one individual at the pulpit leads the thoughts and feelings of the congregation. Whether they follow or not, this common organ of utterance proceeds. The more faithful the audience is to this guidance, and the more effectually adoring love is exercised and developed, the more speedily and certainly will that sovereign affection be attained, out of which is to spring the supreme felicity of the soul. Every appropriate word, then, either of hymn or prayer, should be heard, and its import felt. No expression should be lost to the ear, and no meaning to the heart, any more than should be lost on the learner of music any note from the intent instructor.

Let the duty be brought more closely home by an illustration. Suppose you have a son at school. Imagine word to be brought that this dear child neglects his lessons,— is an idler.

You are surprised, filled with regret, and hasten to the remedy. You admonish, and, if need be, tearfully beseech him. You make the most earnest appeals to his heart not to neglect those exercises by which his powers are to be strengthened, and by which he is to be prepared for business, for respectability, and for greater enjoyment in life. You persevere till he reforms. But oh! parent, give heed to the admonition, and be meek. How much more neglectful and guilty are you, perhaps, than this listless boy, too young to appreciate his privileges! Are not you yourself an idler in another school? And, what is more, do you not set a pernicious example to your own child, and make him and keep him an idler too? The sanctuary of public worship is the great "common school" of the religious affections. Here is an institution whose builder and maker is God; and his gracious providence has brought you thereto. Here Infinite Mercy has appointed, that the noblest capacities of the soul shall be developed and trained into glorious strength, — capacities which most nearly ally us to the angels, and, more than all, enable us to hold communion with the Eternal and the Most High. This seminary especially provides for the culture of that loftiest, holiest attribute of the soul,

— love to God. Here the spirit may drink of the deepest, fullest, sweetest fountain of good, even "joy in the Holy Ghost." Oh, what is the education of intellect, that it may grasp worldly riches, power, or fame, to this education, which, in the present life, bestows the soul's crowning felicity, and prepares for ecstatic love and blessedness in the life everlasting!

We now come to the last and most effectual means of developing the commanded love toward the Lord God: it is prayer. In the stated devotional exercises already considered,— those at the family altar and in the public sanctuary,— this particular blessing, nearness and love to God, would, of course, come in with other subjects of prayer; but, besides these, the individual soul, feeling its own needs, its own faintings and yearnings for the highest good, should alone by itself make earnest and continuous entreaty for the direct aid of the Holy Spirit toward this crowning attainment in the religious life. Truly, if assistance in any case is vouchsafed in answer to supplication, it must be to enhance, with an endless and boundless increase, that love which is the supreme, ineffable delight of the soul, and which, more than any one thing else, was the Creator's end in making man in his own image and likeness. Of all bestowments, those belonging to the inner man are especially to be sought in prayer, and are most bountifully received in answer. Of such favors, nothing can be more readily, tenderly, and largely given than that most perfect of all the perfect gifts from above, — the ability to love the all-gracious Giver himself. What, then, have Christian believers to do but to ask and receive, and to teach and train their children to ask, so that they may be as richly and blessedly answered? It is indeed for the sake of your children, dear friends, that the attempt has been made to show through analogy the highest human capacity, and to present the various methods of development. It is for those you hold dearest that the culture of this capacity has been urged on yourselves. No one can train another with fullest success to love that which he does not himself love. It is for this reason, that, in this special topic of religious education, your own spiritual improvement and felicity have been blended with those of your children. If you have been addressed with more personal directness than may seem befitting, if you have been *preached* to, it was in the sincere and deep conviction, that this "foolishness of preaching" to the parent would best induce practical and effective wisdom toward the child.

In closing, permit one more earnest appeal. Oh for the power adequately to set forth the immensity of blessing to come through entire obedience to "the first and great commandment"! Let all that is beautiful and glorious in creation be displayed to the opened and enraptured vision of one who had been blind from infancy, let the mingled melodies and harmonies of a thousand music-choirs steal upon the unstopped ear of one born deaf, and the ecstasy of delight would but feebly illustrate the deep, the thrilling, the ecstatic bliss, the angel-like joy, which comes from, which indeed is a portion of, love toward God. Range through all the mineral kingdom, and find gems such as royal treasures only can purchase, and present 'them to the dazzled vision, to, the eager acceptance, and you offer nothing of such transcendent worth as this affectional crown of man's whole nature, this more than regal glory, this love towards the Infinite in love.

Should you turn your child out among strangers, should you disinherit him in your will, you could not cause him so wide, deep, dark an abyss of privation as the withholding the nurture of this greatest and strongest, this sovereign of all the loves. A child cast among strangers might find hospitality and friendship, and his own hands might earn a support. If you cut him off from your estate, he might perhaps be saved from indolence and dissipation by such loss, and become rich through his own sufficient energies. But, ah! who can open the inmost, the deepest, the most hidden capacity of his soul, like yourselves? Cold strangers will not do it. The world does it not. The one hour of one day in the week at the Sunday school cannot do it as you might,—you, who are with him from the first opening of his senses, the first thinking of his intellect, the first emotion of his heart; you, whose smile brings his earliest smile, whose love wins forth his earliest love. Yes, you yourselves have opportunities to show him the smile on the countenance of the Highest, and the love which lights up that face of Glory, such as are vouchsafed to no other beings in all the universe beside.

Why is it, that with such a capacity, with such countless incitements to the. unfolding, there is so little love toward God in the Christian world? It is because the poor child has been neglected, and by none comparatively so much as by his own father and mother. It is because these relatives themselves have been neglected by their own parental predecessors. Thus the spiritual desolation has come down, and still continues, just as intellectual barrenness continues from generation to generation where there are no schools or books. Just as some neighborhood remains in vulgar ignorance, so do thousands of families in our Christian civilization remain in irreligiousness, and especially without that inmost and best life of religion, — love toward God. Just as some settlement in the wilderness, or hamlet among the difficult hills, has long waited for the enlightened, the progressive, the successful instructor, so has the lineage of the family been waiting for that parental teacher and renovator, who should inaugurate a new epoch, a new life, a new joy, to those of his name.

Readers, parents, what say you? Shall "the first and great commandment," which left the Saviour's lips nearly two thousand years ago, and has wandered so long amid God's children, and found so little obedience, so little knowledge of it, so little faith in it, so little thought of it, — shall it strike upon your own line, enter your own home, and you, like the rest, continue as those "who, seeing, see not; and, hearing, hear not, and neither do understand"?

Would that these humble arguments and appeals might induce some to feel for themselves and for their children that longing for love toward God, that thirst for a union with him and blessedness in him, which is as the hart's panting for the water-brooks, and which is well expressed in the deep pathos of a prayerful hymn! —

> "Oh that my heart were right with Thee,
> And loved Thee with a perfect love!
> Oh that my Lord would dwell in me,
> And never from his seat remove!
>
> Father, I dwell in mournful night
> Till thou dost in my heart appear:
> Arise, propitious Sun! and light
> An everlasting morning there.
>
> Oh! let my prayer acceptance find,
> And bring the mighty blessing down:
> Eyesight impart, for I am blind;
> And seal me thine adopted son."

Many readers will not need the analogical argument which has been presented. It is enough for them that they are commanded in the divine Word to love the Lord their God supremely. They have the faith that no duty would be there imposed which they are unable to fulfil, although as yet they have not come up to the mark of perfect obedience. Again: they aver that the experiences of thousands of Christians bear sufficient witness to the reality of the blessedness which comes from love to God. "There is no need of tracing analogies," say they; "there is no need of reasoning: here are palpable and incontrovertible facts." But even to these readers it may be replied, that the preceding course of thought may be of use nevertheless. There may come upon them dark seasons of discouragement: even they may question whether apparent facts may not be illusions. They may be tempted even to the thought, that the Scripture language, in its mighty strength, is, after all, but an impressive figure of speech; and their own short-comings and seeming inability to rise to the height required may seem ample confirmation. In the state of mind supposed, will any one aver that our analogical reasoning will not be of some avail in sustaining the sinking spirit?

Still further, these friends will occasionally meet those who distrust all these avowed experiences of love, and consequent satisfactions. Their objections occupy so large a space before their mental sight, that well-substantiated facts are but little seen. How useful, then, to the positive believers in the commands and promises of the Word may be the analogical argument! Its thread can be shown to the doubter to begin in the hidden depths of his own nature, and to run thence up to that perfect love which casteth out fear, and admits only joy and peace. All truths are consistent one with another. It is the part of wisdom, then, to meet the objector on his own ground, with some positive truth fairly acknowledged. Thence, if candid, he may be led to those higher and more interior views, of which, at first, he had no true and clear conception. It is hoped, therefore, that those who may not need this analogical leading to the truth will nevertheless accept it, and apply it to use where it may really be wanted.

And, now, will the friends whose case was attempted to be met in the outset permit me to address them directly once more? You have seen, how that, in the very structure of your mental constitution, there must be the capacity to love God, the source of love; to love him more than any other being can be loved, as being nearest to the soul, not only in relationship, but in that position, as it were, which is most favorable to the closest and most constant intimacy. Why, then, will not your candor, with your reason, accept as positive facts the avowed experiences so numerously presented in the various churches? There are some, who, in their perfect sincerity and unsuspecting simplicity, express their religious fervors without restraint, whether there be few or many to hear. It may be in rude outbursts of prayer, in language unrefined and ungrammatical, or in exultant song without melody; but all this is no evidence that their experience is not real. The jars upon your refinement, the disgusts of your taste, should not blind you to a principle and to a deep want of your own nature. You have but to extend your acquaintance with truly Christian people to find many whose hearts fervently but steadily glow with the greatest love possible to the soul, and who possess a peace which passeth understanding; but they make but little outward demonstration. Perhaps they are hardly distinguished from other respectable and orderly people, who are altogether below their high mark of Christian attainment. With them, truly the kingdom of God cometh without observation. It comes to them more especially unobserved, because there is so much room for it freely to occupy. It is to such believers that you are invited to look for the best evidences of joy in believing. In the inquiry-meeting and the conference-room, there are presented every week the incidents of religious experience, could you be there to hear. The narrators are evidently sincere. The instability of some of them, the returning of some to their past sensual life as the swine to her wallowing, is no proof of insincerity: it is rather a proof of the strength of depraved appetite and passion, and the weakness of the conscience and the will as to better things. Besides those, few or many, who endure but for the moment, who blaze suddenly out and are as suddenly extinguished, how many there are who shine on more and more brightly, even toward the settled and perfect day!

As an illustration of a religious experience, will these friends accept the following trustworthy statement of facts? The narrator was a personal friend of my own, and belonged to one of the most liberal Christian denominations. His profession was that of the law; and he seemed to carry his cool, clear, legal habit of intellect into theological inquiry. In some of his views he was indeed quite radical; yet he was obliged to acknowledge the evidences of his own heart. He was a devoted Sunday-school teacher, and gave me the account in the course of an incidental conversation appertaining to the matters of the school. I may not repeat the exact language of my friend; but I give the facts correctly, I think, as I recall them to memory, at the present writing, after an interval of many years.

"Several years ago, the people of the town in which I resided were proposing to hold a four-days' meeting to produce a revival of religion. I thought that this was not the way to obtain religion, and I very earnestly opposed the measure. I conversed and reasoned with my neighbors a great deal on the subject. Nevertheless, the meetings were held; but I did not attend them myself. In the mean time, I still presented my views in opposition as I had opportunity. I could not, of course, but think a great deal about God, my heavenly Father, and of his character; and read my Bible, from which I drew my own theology, the same as my neighbors did theirs. At length came the sabbath. I did not attend meeting, but staid at home alone. My thoughts were on the great subject which occupied the people generally,— God and religion. All at once, to my utter astonishment, I was taken with a most extraordinary experience. I had a sort of unaccountable influx into my mind of love to God. It was a feeling almost ecstatic, yet calm and still, but deep. At the same time, I felt a peculiar affection toward my neighbors, toward everybody. Indeed, I experienced precisely what my neighbors were holding their four-days' meeting to obtain. I felt what I did not believe myself capable of before. It was an approach toward the fulfilment of the command, 'Thou shalt love the Lord thy God with all thy heart, and with all thy soul, and with all thy mind, and with all thy strength.' I held no more controversy about revivals. I opposed them no longer; for I had a revival of my own."

Such is the statement of my own personal friend, whom I should no more think to doubt than to doubt myself. He made no comments on his experience; he could not himself explain it: he simply offered it as a spiritual fact. To me, however, it shows that an earnest, intense, and continuous contemplation of God, the opening of the soul toward him, without ceasing, from day to day, the yearning after him, the prayer to him, will accomplish in brief space for the adult man or woman, hitherto neglectful, that which ought to have been in process through long educational years. But from this let there be no argument or excuse for neglect. How few there are out of the multitude of the neglected and the neglectful who come at length to this blessed recognition of God, of supreme love toward him, and of the believer's joy! The true doctrine is, to educate the child from the beginning into Christian knowledge, faith, hope, love, and fruition. In this, the aid of the Holy Spirit is to be distinctly and emphatically recognized. All the human faculties are of God's creating; and, without the actual presence and sustaining power of his influence every moment, there would be no body, no mind, no faculties at all. Every thing would fall into nothingness. In respect to those capacities, however, which have immediate relation to spiritual and to heavenly things, it seems to me that there is a direct and immediate action of a heavenly influence, or of the "Holy Spirit." The truth may be illustrated in this way: A child may admire a flower or any other charming object, and say, "Oh, how beautiful! how I love it!" while the parent has but a distant and imperfect sympathy, although the object may be a gift from his own hand. But if that same child shall express an earnest, deep, and most tender love to the parent, and this directly to his listening ear, and with a looking-up to his own bending countenance, he answers back with an earnest, deep, and most tender love in return. He can hardly help it. The inmost, the ever-abiding law of the spiritual nature is, "Ask, and ye shall receive; seek, and ye shall find." This applies to the finite relations, and it equally applies to the infinite. Now, the child is not able of himself, without instruction, to feel the affection toward the heavenly Parent. He must know him and what he has done, and how good, how tenderly kind, he is, before he can love him. The fixed conditions of the child's nature must be regarded in the higher as well as in the lower activities. It is your duty, therefore, parent, to assist your child in his religious development as you would in the discipline of the other several various faculties of his nature. In regard to those exercises appertaining to the highest object of affection, there will be at length a conscious meeting of spirit with spirit, of love with love. The child's heart will find, as it were, the heart of the heavenly Parent, that is, will be conscious of his spirit, with an unspeakable joy, yet all in perfect accordance with that divine order and harmony which run through the universe. When we shall come to understand the laws of the spiritual creation as we do those of the material, we shall say these things must have been thus in the very necessity of things.

Now, I believe in the influx of the very spirit and life of God upon the young soul in its process of religious development. If the child shall be shown God's works, such as the sun, the stars, and the flowers, and thus be made to think lovingly of the greatness and goodness of the Maker, there will steal in upon him a secret heavenly influence, nurturing his germinant affections. In the progress of culture, as God's works in nature, and ways in providence, shall be still further displayed; and especially as his tender compassions in salvation shall be made known; and, still more, as confiding and earnest prayer shall become an habitual exercise,—why shall not the holy regenerating Spirit descend in greater and greater plenteousness, until there shall be a growth "unto a perfect man,—unto the measure of the stature of the fulness of Christ"?

THE CHILD'S FIRST IDEAS OF JESUS.

JESUS CHRIST, next to God the Father, should occupy the child's mind more than any other being in the reception of religious impressions. How important, then, that he should be presented in such a manner as not only to affect the memory, but to touch the heart! Before the child is able to read, he can hear and understand about Jesus. Why, parent, should you not make it a *study* to impart to him his first ideas of the Saviour, and in such a manner as to be engaging, and even delightful, to his little soul? How careful are you to be qualified in every thing appertaining to the business by which you live, and accumulate wealth! But is not your first business, your highest, your best duty, to educate your child, to bring him to God and to a heavenly eternity, and this through Jesus Christ? How careful are you, mother, about household affairs, and especially the comfort of your children! how anxious that they should be cleanly and tasteful at the sabbath school and the church! But how infinitely above all this is your duty to the child's imperishable soul, to the understanding that must have truth, to the memory that must retain it, to the heart that must feel and be moved by its power! It is for you to give the first, deepest, holiest, best ideas of him who said, "Suffer the little children to come unto me, and forbid them not; for of such is the kingdom of God." This yearning tenderness has flowed from that heart of immeasurable love, through the many centuries, a living stream; and now, parent, shall your own heart, like a rock in the way, turn it aside from your child? Or, rather, the Lord Jesus Christ from the heavens at this very moment sends down the holy stream of his grace to these dear subjects of the kingdom; but it must first fall into your own bosom, there to become a well of living water, and thence to spring up into the life, the everlasting life, of your little ones.

A personal appeal has just been made to the mother; but it can hardly be said which parent is most sacredly bound in this momentous charge of the earliest Christian instruction. Let both be faithful. Sometimes one, sometimes perhaps the other, will have better gifts for earliest communication. Let Providence order which shall have the precedence. That same Jesus said, "What God hath joined together, let not man put asunder." It is worthy of note, that this was uttered in connection with the beautiful incident of blessing the children, as recorded in the Gospel of Mark. So let not those conjoined in parentage be put asunder in the training of their common offspring, and especially in that religious culture, which, above every thing else, is of momentous import to the child. Both, therefore, are entreated to make it a special study, how to instruct the child in religion, and especially how to unfold to him the wonderful life, works, and character of Jesus, the Christ. If you are of religious habits, your child must have heard you read of Jesus Christ in the Bible, utter his name in prayer, and speak of him in religious conversation. He must, therefore, necessarily have some faint idea of a person held in reverence and love. Various will be the impressions on different minds of the same age, according to constitutional capacities and idiosyncrasies; but still, at some particular and well-chosen time, you are to impart the first specific instruction concerning this wonderful being, the Son of the "almighty and most merciful God."

Children are, in general, tenderly and deeply interested in infants. Perhaps, therefore, the best method of introducing the learner to the character of Jesus would be to begin with the circumstances of his birth and the condition of his infancy. Let the account of Luke make the commencement. There are the shepherds, keeping watch over their flock by night; then the coming of the angel with his good tidings of great joy; next the sudden presence of the heavenly host, and their song of praise and glory to God. On how many millions of little minds has some Christmas hymn deepened the impression of the Gospel-story! If it could be given to the ear also through the attractive melody of pious lips, there will be an added charm. If possible, then, let the story come, not only through rhyme and rhythm to the little soul, but also through song; but, if this cannot be done by yourself, you may at least softly, sweetly, reverently read the simple narrative in the Bible. How glad will the child be, when he shall be able himself to read, to find with his own eyes, in the book, the very same words which he had first heard from the lips of love!

Then come the scenes of "the babe lying in a manger," and of the wondering shepherds; and, as related in another Gospel, of the star-guided and worshipping wise men, and their singular gifts. The various incidents, however, need not be further indicated. There they are on the sacred page, for the little soul to be filled with them to the full.

Wonder is a mental emotion most easily excited in a child. He loves to wonder. How, then, will the miracles of Jesus lift him up to the mysterious, the incomprehensible; fill him with wonder at the same time that they touch his heart with gratitude, with love, with a deep reverence toward the doer of mighty and marvellous works! A child's sympathy is most easily brought out at the sight of human pain or any kind of trouble. How he will weep, how he will stretch out his own little hands to help, how he will run to and fro to get the assistance of others, when there is some sudden exhibition of suffering! Now, take advantage of this characteristic. Can you not make the child realize the pains, the various sufferings, of those miserable human beings Jesus so compassionately, so tenderly healed? Can you not portray to his mind's eye the Divine Healer, self-possessed and serene, as knowing what he had power to do, and yet, with a countenance of melting pity, bending toward the sufferer? then how, at a touch of his finger, or a few gentle but commanding words, there was instant restoration, — health, strength, rising-up, and walking,— as if there had been a creation anew? Can you not then make him realize the sudden change from utter despair to the intensest joy, as manifested by the face glowing and the eye glistening with emotions such as had never been experienced before, and by the voice tremulous and almost inarticulate in its efforts to pour out the filled bosom's burden of thankfulness to the performer of the wonderful cure? Can you not show to your child also the believing and sympathizing company of disciples, and, besides these, the great multitude of common people, astonished and awe-struck, and bursting forth in utterances of glory to God? Parent, there is no one in the whole compass of time with whose image you could so possess your child's mind, memory, and heart, as with that of Jesus of Nazareth. He transcends all others human by his origin, his character, and his works. He is separate from all others by the sacred names, Son of man, the Christ, the Son of God, Messiah, Immanuel, the Redeemer, the Saviour of the world, the Lord; but, furthermore, he is lifted high above all mere human nature by a mysterious union with the infinite and invisible One, — that Father in heaven, of whom you must have already spoken to your child. "I am in the Father, and the Father in me. He that hath seen me hath seen the Father," said Jesus. "In him dwelleth all the fulness of the Godhead bodily," wrote the apostle. "I am Alpha and Omega, the Beginning and the End, the First and the Last," saith the Lord in the Revelation.

The evangelical record of this, the "Wonderful," is the history of histories in the Book of books. It begins with infant weakness in humble poverty: it ends with the ascending Lord, to whom is given, as he declared, "all power in heaven and in earth." If any thing that was ever told or published should be treated with the educator's most studied and wisest skill, it is these events and circumstances, handed down by the first Christian penmen, and which Providence has laid upon parental responsibility.

The little human being, to whom all the world is new, is of most easy impression. He is in the power of his parents as in that of a superior and irresistible providence, if they so choose. Why shall they not, then, forestall evil with good, little things with those which are truly great and momentous? Why shall they not make Jesus Christ occupy so large a place in the opening mind, make his image so beautiful, so attractive, so sweetly charming, and so great and glorious, that every other one of human form shall seem in comparison small, dim, and utterly insignificant?

A few stanzas of a lofty hymn, borne upon the strains of a grand old tune, come echoing along the chambers of memory from loved voices heard in earliest years. Let them have a place here. Perhaps they may be caught up anew in many homes, and wafted melodiously into opening memories there, and go sounding on, calling back, ever and anon, the wandering affections to their fealty.

> " All hail the great Immanuel's name!
> Let seraphs prostrate fall:
> Bring forth the royal diadem,
> And crown him Lord of all.
>
> Let countless angels strike the lyre,
> And low before him fall,
> Who tune to love their holy choir,
> And crown him Lord of all.

> Let every tribe of every tongue,
> All creatures, great and small,
> Loud swell this universal song,
> And crown him Lord of all." *

---

* The hymn has been somewhat altered from the original in the course of time, and the improvements (if so they may be called) have been adopted here. Opportunity is now taken to say, that allusion to any specific doctrine of salvation has been purposely avoided. It was thought that the object of this treatise would best be answered by general incitements to love and honor God and the Son, to which none could object, rather than by any sectarian peculiarities. It is supposed, however, that the quotations from Scripture, such as here introduced, would be acceptable to all denominations, each one making its own interpretation as to the pre-eminence signified.

THE BIBLE.

Of all the books in the world, that which your child should love most is the Bible. He should not only reverence it, but he should have for it a profound affection. As you would seek the best interests of your child, as you would have the Rock which is ever higher than he always in sight, through all the storms of temptation, the mists of false doctrine, and the darkness of depravity, take care how you show to him, and keep before him from the earliest, the word of God.

There are some observances, in regard to the mere keeping of the Book, which might have a salutary effect on the mind. The large family Bible should be kept in some particular place assigned: it should never lie carelessly about here or there in the dust, like any other ordinary publication of the passing times. I would even here have a case or cabinet made for it purposely,—a tabernacle you may call it, if you so please, — with glass in the door, through which the volume could be seen, separate from all other volumes. This tabernacle should be placed in the family-room, where it could be looked up to with reverence, even as the Israelites looked toward the tabernacle within which abode the Shechinah of Jehovah. From this, every morning and evening, the Word should be taken and read by the father-priest amid the assemblage of his beloved. Then prayers should be made as if inspiration, winging the soul upward, had been caught from its sacred pages. Let each child have a care that his own Bible (for he should have one), appropriated to his private use, shall be kept with the utmost regard to neatness. Let the sacred volume be always spoken of with respect; yes, with reverence.

Never associate with any passage of the holy Word any ludicrous incident. Never suffer, if you can possibly help it, any person, no matter how old in years or high in position, to narrate a laughable mistake or blunder made by some one in reading the Bible. Such an anecdote, once falling upon the receptive mind of a child, will hardly be cleansed out of memory in this life: it may not be in the life to come. He who thus defiles a child's memory, commits an abomination in the holiest temple of religion upon earth, even in that soul whose builder and maker is God. For myself, I should rather have the adornments of my house defaced, my windows broken, my very garments wrested from my children's backs by ruffians, than to have a courteous friend, in the agreeable interchanges of conversation, associate, as I have known it happen, the ludicrous and the laughable with God's holy and eternal truth.

We now return to the question, How shall the child be made to love the Bible? There will be a constitutional difference between one child and another which may help or hinder an interest. There are children who will love to read, or hear you read, those mysterious things which even you yourself do not understand. There are those who will read the wonderful Apocalypse with a deep fascination. The majority, however, probably, would not thus be interested. You must find out what the peculiar taste is, and the accessible point. Children delight in narrative: read to them an account of the miracles of Jesus, also the parables. Read the story of Joseph, and other touching things in the Old Testament. Read whatever they love to hear about. Do not read a great deal at a time. It is better that your exercise should stop before the interest at all subsides, than continue beyond it. As you proceed, make explanations. If your heart is in the work of your child's education, you will find yourself able to do this, and you will grow in ability. Be careful that your child shall remember no severe language or harsh disposition of your own in connection with your Bible-reading. When he shall think of the Bible, let it be mostly as of the heavenly Father, and the loving Jesus, and the beautiful angels, and of good men; or, if he must think of bad men, let it be as of those whom the loving Father and the blessed influences of the blessed Book would have made better. If you shall be judicious, you can induce him to commit to memory, in the course of years, a large portion of the sacred writings, without the feeling of an unpleasant task. Some of the beautiful narratives in the Gospels, also the parables, and very many of the precepts, might be stored up in mind. Indeed, the whole Sermon on the Mount might be thus treasured up. The Psalms particularly, or selections therefrom, and also from the Prophets, might be committed to memory, especially such portions as are adapted to be chanted in religious worship. If there is any one thing which is now wanted as a new feature in religious education, it is the training of children to chant the holy Word. Let the older members of the family learn to chant. Those yet quite too young to do it can sing in the spirit; and perhaps their own little voices will drop into the broad stream of melodies as they find the Word thus sweetly falling on their ear from other lips. Could the sacred language float to their hearing at church from the choir and the congregation, how easily could they then be led to commit to memory the words which had been made charmingly melodious! Some very strenuously object to children's learning by rote what they do not understand. Hence they would have only those simple and practical precepts committed to memory which shall be at the time altogether intelligible. But the Sacred Scriptures, in their origin, import, and use, can bear no comparison with school textbooks, in which dry terms and rules are generally so distasteful. These mainly have to do with the bare intellect. The Scriptures concern not so much the head as the heart. At first, indeed, the intellect merely may be engaged in memorizing, because the understanding is not yet able to present the selected passages to the affections; but, even in these cases, the parental givers and hearers of the lesson may distil their own hearts like dew upon it, thus making it of easy and sweet acceptance. They can tell the learner of its hidden riches, which shall come forth to sight at a maturer age as come the green blades and the grain from seed buried in the soft mould of the ground.

Some of the Bible names, though not at first signifying much to the young mind, still have a beauty about them, which will make them a blessing to the memory, without any burden. This is peculiarly true of a few geographical names; such as Judæa, Jerusalem, Zion, Bethlehem, Sharon, Hermon, Tabor, Carmel, Lebanon, and others. There is melody in the very sound. How many of these names are woven into spiritual song, to charm the sense, if not to soften or uplift the spirit! But it is supposed that these Scripture names have a specific meaning, which made them peculiarly appropriate in their first application to objects. Could these pristine significations be found, as at some future period they may be, how then would these beautiful words, and indeed many other names of holy writ, open like a rich fruitage from those receptacles of memory where they have been dropped!

I believe myself that in the Sacred Scriptures is the inspiration of God, and that the very angels draw near as it is read, and especially as it is read by children. Their evil affections are less developed than those of adults; they are yet in comparative innocency; so that the good angels can come nearer, or rather angels have not yet been discouraged, and compelled to go away.

Children now are trained from their earliest ability of voice and tune to sing and perform hymns adapted to their age. Soon they are able to join in the congregational singing at church. Indeed, a large portion of the hymns sung in ordinary worship are intelligible to children, so that they can sing with the spirit and understanding also. Why shall they not also be taught to chant the inspired Word? With this engaging accompaniment, how easily would they commit to memory devotional parts of the Psalms and the Prophets! These would be a richer treasure to their memories than volumes of the profane poetry of the world. There is no objection to reading, and committing to memory, the pure productions of genius, whether of prose or poetry; but, beside all these, like the vital fluid in the body, or a finer essence within this, there should be the *divine Word* in memory and heart. Its truths should be the vitalizing essence of all other knowledge and literature. Those not experienced have no possible conception of the spiritual, living influences from the word of God.

One reason why parents set so little value on the Scriptures, for themselves and their children, is because they have no conception of the virtue, the power, which go forth from them. They look upon them as they look upon other writings, estimating them according to their notions of external and artistic beauty, or the evidences of their historic authenticity and genuineness. They have no idea of the living spirit which ever abides with and moves these cloudy and multiform chariots of language. A fact will best illustrate the sweet, the heavenly influences of the Word. One well known to the writer, between whose home and whose business lay a tract of naked ground, rough and unsightly, together with streets occupied by the uncleanly abodes of a foreign population, their untidy children prominent and noisy along the thresholds, adopted the following method of using the time of his daily travel to his employment. He copied upon little cards portions of the Psalms and Prophets. These he committed to memory on his way. He avers that the unsightly things which before pained his eye as he passed, were now, as it were, shut out of sight; and the distance was hardly thought of. His feet seemed almost to be lifted up, and wings given to his body, as he now went to his day's duties. It was the sweet, delicious influence from the Word that lifted him up and bore him along. He walked through heavenly scenes now, rather than along the rude, disorderly, disagreeable ways of ignorance, poverty, and sin. This fact will illustrate the power that may be exercised by God's word through all the hard, rough passages of human life. It is for you, parents, to say whether your children shall have such comfort, such consolation, such inspiration, or not. Indeed, however easy may be their lot, however calm their life's journey, passages from the Word treasured in memory will be lights along the way to cheer and bless; clear shinings, such as cannot be estimated by those who themselves have had no experience.

There are many lonely hours which can be alleviated by no human companionship, when no book is at hand, and when outward objects have no interest to the eye. At these times, if the memory shall be well stored with the riches of knowledge, there will be resources which outward circumstances, unless they shall be quite painful, cannot diminish or dim. Many a wakeful hour on the bed at night might be made devout with worship, and bring the angels sweetly into fellowship, by the perusal of Psalm or Gospel written on the memory. Sleep might come, and catch the spirit from the midst of holy writ, and bear it in vision to angelic scenes and to heavenly places in Christ Jesus. Such things have been, and they may always be, under similar blessed conditions. But in the season of sickness, the body prostrate, the hands strengthless, and the eye failing, then how might the treasured Word flow like a river of life from the memory out into the heart, bearing a refreshment and a dewy peace, compared with which all the geniuses and literatures of the world would be but as a parching drought!

There may be passages from the beautiful literature of one's own language or the ancient classics, which the mind may run over in these hours, and bring up freshly to view; but all such choice selections meet the mind's eye generally with the effect to present external beauty, artistic excellence. They are gazed upon, as it were, like a picture, a statue, fair and perfect, but, comparatively at least, cold and lifeless. They afford but little life, power, efficiency, to the soul. Indeed, how few there are, even of those liberally educated or highly cultivated, who resort systematically to historic, poetic, and classic remembrances to relieve the tedium of lonely hours! How different it is, or might be, with the treasuring-up of God's various Word in the memory! In the first place, the Scripture itself makes it a duty to think of God; to have him in mind before all other beings. In the next place, this very Scripture, rightly understood, will show that this having God in mind, this consciousness of him, will be the source of the highest possible felicity to the soul. Next, the very Word itself will be the very best possible medium of receiving the idea of God, and of being filled with a full consciousness of his character, and with a love for him as a Father, as the most tenderly loving being in the universe; and, finally, there will come with this Word, as it is committed to memory, a sweet influence, a delicious influx, from God himself or the Holy Spirit, which none but those who have experienced can know.

As early as good judgment will allow, and

continuously, let your child's memory be stored with these riches, which never take wings except to bear their possessor heavenward, and which no man, nor all the world together, can take away. Although he may be learned in all the lore of many nations and ages, and though all the sciences of nature shall be as familiar to him as the alphabet, yet, on the bed of mortal sickness and at the dying hour, passages from the Book of books will take precedence of every thing else. The incitements to trust, the confirmations of faith, the promises to hope, presented by the inspired Word, will be worth all the libraries and memorized learning of the world. How many of the earth's mightiest in wealth, learning, intellect, and genius, have at last been glad to repose the spirit on some of the Psalms, as the wasted and sore frame might repose on the couch and pillow made soft and easy by the hands of affection! How have they come down from the world's pride to sit at the feet of Jesus in the Gospels, in the utmost humbleness and docility; indeed, to cast themselves upon his bosom like little children on a parent's breast, believing this to be the safest place for refuge and peace!

NOTES.

I.

It was the author's purpose to add a section on the culture of the Conscience; but the space left was found quite too limited for the largeness and importance of the topic. This point of discipline has been so egregiously neglected, and the consequences have been so enormously destructive, that a considerable treatise, instead of a few pages, seemed requisite to do it justice. In fact, in the effort to prepare the article intended, the subject assumed such magnitude, it ran out into so numerous ramifications, and brought to view such a multitude of illustrative incidents, that the worker was overwhelmed with his materials, and knew not what best to select to make the necessary abbreviation. Friendly readers are therefore besought patiently to wait for a much better service than could be performed at the close of a volume already quite too large for convenience in these crowded times. It is proposed, Providence favoring, to present at a future opportunity, in a separate work, some suggestions on Right and Wrong, and the education of that vicegerent of God, and sovereign on the soul's judgment-seat,—the Conscience.

II.

In a note at the bottom of page 17, it is intimated that something would be said about meetings for educational discussion which have been held in various parts of the country. After that note was printed, the plan of the work was considerably changed, so that an account of the meetings referred to was necessarily excluded. Their practicability and valuable use will be considered at some future time, if the author shall be permitted to carry out his plans of publication. He would take this opportunity to make known, that he has a large quantity of educational matter on hand,—the accumulation of many years,—which he hopes to present eventually for public use.

INDEX.

	Page.
Action, attractive to infant curiosity	215
Adulteration of goods remedied by education	150
Advantage of good judgment as to size	160
Agricultural lessons	228
Ambition and demagogism, how sometimes originated	82
Amusing the baby	75
An abuse of nature	140
Analogical argument, the use of an	325-7
Analogical reasoning about love to God	296
Anecdotes and incidents in illustration, 18, 29, 31, 35, 38, 47, 49, 58, 86, 87, 90, 94, 100, 101, 107, 111, 118, 164, 167, 173, 180, 330,	351
Animals, knowledge of	175
Apparel of children, abuse and use of	87
Appeal to the parent to study how to teach	335
Arithmetic, where and how it should begin	196
Bad companions, how to keep children from	120
Beating down prices before children	98
Beginning of intellectual development	135
Benevolence and true usefulness, how taught	103
Best end of the bargain, the worst end	98
Bible, child's love and reverence for the	344
Birds, as objects of interest and study	175
Blessedness of love toward God	322
Bodily health cared for, moral health neglected	20
Books on family education, what booksellers say of	16

INDEX.

	Page.
Books, use of	272
Books explaining nature, mentioned in a foot-note	182
Boxes and shelves in the schoolroom, for a new use	142
Brain, care of the health of	76
Business-men, the way they learn arithmetic	210
Cabinet of minerals begun by a child	174
Capacity to love God to the degree expressed in the command, analogically presented	295
Care over household things, how taught	200
Care over domestic animals	202
Care of infancy and childhood considered a petty business	21
Casual events, notice of	233
Catalogue of petty parental inflictions	50
Causality and its questions	179
Chanting the Holy Word	350
Cheapening an almanac, amusing instance of	100
Chief purpose of this world	3
Child-traveller after curiosities	152
Child keeping playthings and clothes in order	259
Children's interest in the miracles	339
Christmas-hymns	338
Ciphering with real profit at home	211
City young man and the country preacher	87
Clergyman's children	130
Closet-scene, mother and child	48
Clouds, a school-boy's philosophy about	180
Color, faculty of, how cultivated	163
Color-game	164
Commandment, the first and great	293
Commandment, the first and great, disbelief in the literal truth of the language of	293
Committing the Scriptures to memory	292
Commodities at home, education in	148
Compass, the use of, in education	189
Companionship, bad, how avoided	120
Concentration, power of, improved	207
Conscience, first dawning of	36
Conscience, discipline of	244
Contrast in a child's possibilities	3

INDEX. 361

	Page.
Convention for horses and poultry	17
Corn, beans, and peas, as exercises in counting	206
Counting-game	198
Creator, first knowledge of	279
Dangerous exposure of the young	19
Dangers of modern society	19
Deceit and double-dealing of both children and parents	102
Defect in personal soundness and beauty, care against	18
Degree in which we can love God	298
Democracy in the family	39
Dendrology learned incidentally	206
Differences between one person and another in noticing incidents	216
Discipline, penal, various mild forms of	51
Discipline, how it may begin	225
Discipline of the time-piece	253
Dissipation of a little child	81
Dissipation of youth in cities, how occasioned	85
Distances, learning how to measure	190
Distinguished mineralogist, how he first became interested in his science	173
Distinguished men	270
Duplicity and deceit in bargains	97
Earliest object of a child's notice	163
Early moral symptoms fearfully premonitory	22
Early attention to the time-faculty	252
Eating, excessive, destructive effects of, on children	82
Economy and saving, practical teaching of	146
Economical idea	200
Education by parents, estimation of, compared with other interests	15
English nobility, their children's food	83
Entomology for the young	177
Errand-doing on all-fours	103
Eventuality, power of	215
Evil, the child's capabilities of	4
Evils of society traceable to parental neglect	13
Example of a distinguished parental educator	33

INDEX.

	Page.
Faculty of individuality, what it is, and how cultivated	155
Falsehoods, people inured to them, and submit	222
Family government, some have a natural gift for	37
Family ciphering	211
Father taking pastime with his children	230
Father and mother conjoined in religious teaching	337
Fictitious literature improved	237
Fire at night, readiness to escape	260
Firmness, culpable lack of, in the parent	40
Firmness with mildness will be respected, and will prevail	52
Fishes affording mental nutriment	178
Florence Nightingale, her philanthropy	69
Flowers	166
Food, philosophy of	79
Foreigners shocked at the irreverence and unruliness of our youth	38
Form, faculty of, and its culture	158
Fourth of July celebrated at home	122
Francis, the idiot	107
Gatherings for any thing but home-education	16
Geography, where and how the study of, should begin	185
Gifts, as tokens for affection	117
God's provision for the child's safety and culture	7
God, his character	65, 67
God, name of	280
God, name of — manner of speaking it	284
God, qualities and attributes of	285
God as a Father	286
God as seen in various objects of Nature	289
Gossip, together with imagination, its harmfulness	221
Government, grounds of parental	27
Government, first occasion for	27
Grains, observation of	167
Grandmother, the excuse of a, for her daughter	44
Help of boys and girls in a family	104
Henry Ware, jun., extracts from his hymn on prayer	315, 316
Hiring children to obey	45
History of the divine dealings	310

INDEX.

	Page.
Holy Spirit aiding religious love	332
Holy Spirit, different operations of	328
Holy Spirit, interesting case of individual experience	329
Home, how a new, may be considered	11
Honor and honesty	101
Honorable, a singular use of the title	101
Household lessons in eventuality	226
How not to get lost	188
Hymn from Dr. Watts	310
Idle young men and young women	105
Infantile impulses	28
Infantile activity	150
Ignorance of the names and natures of trees	169
Individualizing faculty improved by counting objects	207
Individualizing	155
Industrial efforts of a little child	139
Insight into various trades and pursuits	229
Insect curiosities	176
Instance of a child's keen observation	169
Instinct of the brute parent never abused	40
Instinctive human parental love, use and abuse of	40
Instinctive observation in a child	232
Intellect, premature awakening of	73
Intellect, disproportionate strength and activity of	75
Inventories and appraisals of property; to make them, how taught	204
Irish woman's terrible threat to her child	49
Irreverence, growing, among the young	38
Jesus, the child's first idea of	335
John Quincy Adams, his going-to-sleep verse	317
Judgment as to the quantities of things, how improved	199
Judgment, how a good, comes	268
Knowledge, how a child gets much of, without books	137
Knowledge of wood and timber important, and how obtained	171
Language of the Scriptures, influence of, in the child's memory	290

	Page.
Lawrence, Amos, his love of doing good	68
Leaves, different kinds of	170
Letter, Rev. Mr. Northrop's, on object-teaching	274
Lies and scandals, how they may originate and grow	220
Literature in certain emergencies	353
Little girl helping her mother in a peculiar way	164
Living creatures compared with pictures, as objects of interest to children	175
Lofty hymn and grand old tune, their power	342
Loss and gain	146
Love and labor for others, genuine happiness of	65
Love to the neighbor, philosophy of	69
Love to God, means of development of	302
Man, his capabilities and possibilities	3
Manufacturing lessons	228
Maps, what the mind's eye should see on them	195
Maternal associations (foot-note)	17
Maternal self-possession illustrated	125
Meal-time punishment	129
Measuring implements for children	159
Measuring time by the sun	253
Melody of some Bible-names	349
Memorial of the heavenly Father	312
Mental hospitality	131
Microscope for family use	177
Minerals, children's knowledge of	172
Minute traits of a landscape to be observed	186
Mischief, the child's work; use of it	29
Missionaries, where they should begin	110
Money, early love and abuse of	93
Moon and stars, medium of religious instruction	228
Mother's blessedness in her babe	67
Mother's toil for the child's pleasure	42
Nation, present state of our, and why so	242
Nature's works and ways to be noticed	231
Neatness, personal	262
Neglect of parental preparation for the child's training	12
New intellectual discipline	223

INDEX. 365

	Page.
News of all sorts, craving appetite for; its effect	239
New-Testament attractions	291
No and yes of the weak parent	40
Nothing to do as a punishment	52
Number of criminals in the United States	14
Number, the relation of, considered	196

Object-game ... 156
Object-teaching, letter from the Agent of the Massachusetts Board of Education ... 274
Obligation, peculiar, of parents for their children's spiritual welfare ... 323
Observing faculties, hints toward the early culture of ... 150
Observation, actual, practical advantage of ... 194
Observing power, differences in the ... 216
Old people's facetious complaint ... 39
Old merchant busy still ... 106
Order, special faculty of ... 256
Order, how to discipline it ... 258
Order in household matters ... 261
Order in boys ... 262
Our Father in heaven as a title of the Creator ... 286
Out-doors ... 202

Parents may get learning from little children ... 154
Parents' opportunity for training the child to love God ... 323
Parents both united in the religious training of their child ... 336
Parentage, solemn responsibility of ... 7
Partisan calumnies checked by what means ... 241
Pattern mother's weakness ... 47
Perceptive faculties, general remarks on ... 266
Persian bishop's remark to a young lady ... 38
Persevere till you subdue an offender ... 52
Phenomena of Nature instructive to children ... 179
Philanthropic little boys ... 111
Picture of neglected morals ... 13
Pictures of animals delightful to infants ... 175
Place, or geography at home ... 185
Playthings and clothes, care of ... 259
Poetry, religious ... 309

	Page.
Points of the compass to be learned	188
Poor imposed on in trade — new remedy for it	145
Prayer, private	315
Prayer for ability to love God	320
Prayerful hymn	325
Prevalent ignorance about natural phenomena	180
Pride of position at school	89
Primary selfishness	71
Promptitude, disastrous lack of	251
Providential pre-arrangement for parental government	35
Public movements and spectacles	235
Punctuality as to promises	250
Punishment, corporal	50
Psalms and Prophets, their allusions to God's works and ways	290
Rat and mouse made something of	176
Reading, its multifariousness	15
Reason *why* not always to be given	35
Recollections, vivid ones important	269
Record of failings and amendments, its peculiar advantage	53
Reform in newspapers	240
Relation of the earthly parent to the heavenly Parent	55
Religious relations of the parent to the child	55
Religious faculties must be used to be developed	305
Religious remembrances, interesting case of	58
Religious experiences	328
Remarkable instance of a mother's influence	58
Republic, a monarchy the foundation of a	40
Resort of earth's mightiest at last	353
Resource for the lonely night-watches	353
Rocks, peculiar and beautiful objects of nature	173
Rosary of the Church universal	308
Rules overruled in parental weakness, — consequences	30
Russian czars, the children of, as to luxuries	84
Sabbath-worship, fidelity in performing	318
Sacred writings committed to memory	347
Sailors' power of sight	157
Sanctuary, the " common school " of religion	319
Scales for children's use	162

INDEX.

	Page.
School-girl's amusing notion about clouds and rain	180
Schooling which is profitable	142
Seeing things and actions, and describing them just as they are	223
Selfishness, how children are trained to	70
Selfishness, education a cause of	92
Self-love, how strengthened from the beginning	72
Setting the table, occasion of a lesson	226
Shells, what might be done with, on a winter's day	178
Showing off a child's learning	92
Sick little boy, the beautiful play of	113
Sickness, how solaced and refreshed	353
Sister at baby-tending endangered	78
Singular birthday present from a child	118
Size, faculty of, how cultivated	159
Snakes and worms, scientifically reputable	176
Spoiled child, what he does	42
Stage-coach ride with a school-girl	167
Star, child's first impression of	288
Stratagem and deception in family government	45
Stones by the wayside, objects of interest	174
Stones in the walls	174
Style of living as an occasion of vanity and pride	88
Success in life, early preparation for	9
Sun, the first object by which to convey the idea of God	281
Sun, illustrating what a parent should be	53
Swapping among boys	97
Sympathy wanted by the infant	153
Table, children at	127
Tasteful dress for a child	88
Temper of a child injured by over-eating	85
Temper, irritability of, in parent and child	123
Things not to be touched by a child	152
Things should go with words in teaching a child to count	197
Threat, horribly ludicrous	48
Threatening, and not performing	47
Throne, the strongest, in all the world; what it is	8
Time, faculty of, discipline in regard to	248
Time wasted in talk	249
Tour of the room by a child on all-fours	29

INDEX.

	Page.
Trees, knowledge of	168
Trying to govern, time foolishly spent in	44
Turning over a new leaf by the mother	31
Two beings who cannot be escaped	246
Two individuals chosen out of a thousand millions	11
Unimportant incidents, the use of, in training	234
Unmannerly children at table	127
Vanity in apparel	87
Various aspects of Nature generally as to color	165
Vegetable appearances particularly	166
Victoria and the royal heirs	83
Why people are so ignorant of Nature	181
Watts's Divine Songs	309
Weight, faculty of, how cultivated	161
Well-governed child, how happy he is	44
Wild youth, whither sent for correction	32
Willis, extract from a poem of	288
Witness in a court-room	219
Where family order or disorder usually begins	28
Whipping, with what spirit it should be done, if necessary	50
Who most benefited by a favor	66
Wonder, a faculty of the child exercised in respect to the miracles and life of Jesus	339
Word of God, its vitalizing and uplifting influence	351
Worker, the Infinite One	105
Worship, social, domestic, and public	317
Worship, philosophy of	313
Worth of character, admirable example in respect to	90
Wrong-doer sent to bed in the daytime	52

www.ingramcontent.com/pod-product-compliance
Lightning Source LLC
Chambersburg PA
CBHW031419230426
43668CB00007B/364